Facets of Life

*What I Didn't Expect When
I was Expecting*

By Lori Clark Weatherly

Copyright © 2011 by Lori Clark Weatherly

Facets of Life
What I Didn't Expect When I was Expecting
by Lori Clark Weatherly

Printed in the United States of America

ISBN 9781613791462

All rights reserved solely by the author. The author guarantees all contents are original and do not infringe upon the legal rights of any other person or work. No part of this book may be reproduced in any form without the permission of the author. The views expressed in this book are not necessarily those of the publisher.

Unless otherwise indicated, Bible quotations are taken from The New King James Version (NKJV). Copyright © 1979, 1980, 1982 by Thomas Nelson, Inc.; The HOLY BIBLE, NEW INTERNATIONAL VERSION. Copyright © 1973, 1978, 1984 by International Bible Society. Used by permission of Zondervan Publishing House; The Holy Bible, King James Version (KJV). Copyright © 1972 by Thomas Nelson Inc., Camden, New Jersey 08103; and The Living Bible (TLB). Copyright © 1971 by Tyndale House Publishers, Wheaton, Illinois 60187.

Cover by Madella Jordan shutupandsmilephotography.com

www.xulonpress.com

Dedication

In honor of our precious baby boy Matthew, I dedicate this book to my loving husband, Ronnie (RW), to our incredible boys, Nathan and William, and to our families who have supported and encouraged us through the darkest of times, celebrated with us at the most joyous occasions and loved us through them all. To every hurting heart out there that has had to overcome the death of a child, I say to you, I understand. Know that God has not forgotten you, He will never forsake you and with Him, ALL things are possible.

Acknowledgments

To my husband, Ronnie, you have been the most amazing husband through our journey of life together. When we said for better or for worse…we had no idea we would live it within our first 10 years of marriage. Thank you for being the man of God that He has called you to be and for loving me "unconditionally." To my boys, Nate and Will, I love you. Every day of my life I will fight to be the best mama I can be for you two. You are pure treasures for me and I am so very blessed to have you both. To Matthew, I love you, you are my Sunshine!

To my parents, Charles and Sylvia, thank you for the foundation that you gave to me and for being the parents that believed in the truth of Proverbs 22:6. Thank you for allowing me to see God's grace in your lives as I grew up, for teaching me faith, and for the many hours you have wept on your knees for me and my family. I love you truly.

To my Father and Mother-in-law, Ron and Rose, thank you both for setting that example in Ronnie's life that he has followed in establishing a loving and close relationship with our boys. Thank you for being there for him when I was in the hospital and in those fragile days after and always. I love you both.

To my sisters, Charlene and Lynette, thank you for being willing to do whatever it took to share this burden with me. Thank you for making sure my boys are always taken care of when I have a doctor's appointment or you know I am just having a bad day. You are the best sisters and I don't know what I would have done or do without you.

To Todd and Lynette, thank you for spending so much time with Matthew at the funeral home while I was in the hospital, and most of all for making the molds of his hand and foot for me... Carol, thank you for the inspiration to do so! It is the most valuable and precious thing that I possess. (I am holding Matthew's sweet little crystal hand on the book cover.)

To my brothers, Chuck and Eddie, thank you for always wanting to protect me and hug me when I need it. Thank you for the phone calls after my doctor's appointments to check on me. I am a lucky little sister to have you both, even when y'all aggravate the stew out of me!

To my sisters-in-law, Rhonda and Rita, thank you for being there to help Ronnie on the days he needed to know you were there and Anthony, thank you for always checking on my feet!

To Mrs. Catherine Parker, thank you for being my grandmother here on earth, and a great-grandmother to my boys. We sure needed you and are so thankful for the time we had you in our lives. Now that you are in heaven, you can tell Matthew all about us and make sure my room is really glitzed up! I sure miss and love you!

To my close friends, thank you all for the days you prayed relentlessly over me and for the hours of encouragement that you poured into me. Thank you for the cards, the emails, the flowers and the meals that were prepared for my family. I am so blessed to have each one of you in my life and I am forever grateful.

To Mrs. Clara Young and Mrs. Ann Street, "honorary mamas" in my life, you are both so special to our family and we love you.

To my dear friend, Shawn Welter, we have been through a lot together! We both have seen how out of tragedy comes such beauty, and at just 6 weeks apart... our little "Will" and "Grace." Thank you for being my best friend and for showing up on my door step September 10th with that basket full of blessings that would prove to come full circle between us! I love you girl!

To two of my incredible doctors at Ochsner, Dr. Jack Winters and Dr. David Margolin, thank you for your compassion and for helping me learn to live again with your knowledge and capability of performing the surgeries needed to improve the quality of life for me. Thank you for being persistent and not giving up on me when I was such a mess. Susan, thank you for your kindness always.

Thanks to all of the blood donors who gave blood in my name when I was in ICU. I will never forget your acts of kindness. It was very humbling to read all of the names and cards knowing that each one of you stood in a line to give your blood so that I and others could live. May God bless you.

To my photographer and friend, Madella Jordan, thank you for capturing the pure beauty in moments that we will treasure for a lifetime. Thank you for giving a mother something so priceless in a photograph that would exhibit such 'reflections' in our "Facets of Life."

To our attorney and friend, R. Hayes Johnson, thank you for your wise counsel, your friendship, and most of all for the compassion that you have shown to us over the years. May God bless you and your beautiful family.

To Danita Holladay, thank you for making that phone call, and not giving us a reason to say no! We are so thankful for your obedience to God and for helping to complete God's will in our lives! What an incredible journey that you have taken us on! Words of gratitude will never be enough!

Thanks to everyone who has done the behind the scenes work and helped me bring this book to completion: Dr. Larry Keefauver and Pam McLaughlin at YMCS for their copyediting and writing suggestions; to Scott and the staff at Xulon for seeing it through to publication. A special thank you to Pam, not just my editor, but my fellow praying mama whom was a Godsend to me and to this book; you are clearly an incredible gift to have on this most special project in my life.

To God, I give thanks and glory for all of the wonderful things He has done and continues to do. He has been my source of strength, my hope, my peace and my comfort. Thank you, God, for Your grace, Your mercy and Your unfailing love. May Your will be done in my life and in the lives of those that read this book.

Foreword

by Nathan L. Weatherly age 10

My mom has had many tests in her faith. God has pulled our family out of many harsh situations and we have learned from them. I was only 5 years old when my mom went into the hospital to have my baby brother. We thought my mom was going to pass away. It was a very sad but joyful moment because I had a little brother now and he was going up to heaven. The day of his funeral, I remember my Paw Paw speaking, but I don't remember what he said. I do remember being able to hold my baby brother for the last time until I get to heaven.

My mom has overcome many, many illnesses and struggles, but that shows how powerful God is. This has tremendously impacted my faith and belief in God. Now I know for sure He is real because of the things He has done for my family and all the people around us.

Almost 6 years later, my mom is doing great because God gives her the power to overcome her illnesses, and helps her with her pain, even when it is really intense. It is a miracle my mom is not in a wheelchair. She has to exercise everyday to keep from losing anymore muscle in her legs and must persevere through pain while she does.

Every time my mom has to go to the hospital or have surgery, I get nervous because I don't know the outcome. I have learned to leave the results up to God.

Because God sent His only Son to die on the cross for us, we can be saved no matter who we are. God can help you get through trials and struggles, just as God has helped us. If your family is going through a difficult time, hang on to your faith. If you are not right with God, I hope you believe me knowing that the power of God is always with us.

A verse that I always keep in my heart that helps keep my head up is Philippians 4:13.

I can do all things through Christ who strengthens me.

I know the power of God because I have lived through some pretty hard stuff. I have suffered and I have seen my parents suffer, too. But I have also seen how faith can affect any situation. This book will surely bump up your faith and let you see just what God can do!

Table of Contents

Introduction	Pain Is…	xv
Chapter One	What I Didn't Expect When I was Expecting	17
Chapter Two	An Unexpected Storm – Katrina	27
Chapter Three	The Unexpected Emotions of First Holidays	40
Chapter Four	Matthew's First and Second Birthdays	54
Chapter Five	"GOD'S WILL" became "OUR WILL."	66
Chapter Six	Barna Belles - The Great Encouragers	77
Chapter Seven	The Fear Factor	89
Chapter Eight	The Disappointment Factor	101
Chapter Nine	Nathan	108
Chapter Ten	Happiness is Circumstantial, Joy is God-Given	120
Conclusion	One Day At A Time	129
About the Author		137
RAK	Random Acts of Kindness	139

Introduction

Pain Is...

P ain is what I have endured for the sake of survival, mentally and physically. Pain is silent. Pain is hard. Pain is self destructing. Pain is the removal of the quietness in my inner being. Living in chronic pain tempts me to be envious of those I see walking and talking all around me. But pain is also the endless echo in my heart that says it is not just me that hurts. There are others out there that are also in constant pain. Pain drives me to my passion, my passion for compassion.

If I want to stand, I have to face the pain and fight it both physically and emotionally. It is clearly a choice... one I have to make daily. Some days I have made bad choices, some days I have made good ones. With each choice comes a consequence or a reward; a victory or a defeat. With each choice comes the desire to make a better one next time that will benefit the mind, the body, the soul and the spirit and promote the faith that lies within. No one would willingly exchange joy and peace for sadness and heartache but the choices we make reflect where we have placed our faith and set the stage for how we handle the pains of life.

We have been told God never fails and that He loves us and wants only what is best for us. We say we believe it and maybe even tell others they need to trust God in their trials and tribulations. But then it happens to us. I have been in that place where I have thought God failed me. It is never easy to comprehend why life has dealt an unexpected blow or sent an unexpected storm. When the unexpected hit me and my family, I had days the faith that had always sustained me seemed so distant that I just couldn't seem to grab on to it. I could see myself trying to with all that I had, yet it seemed to slip right through my fingers leaving me holding only despair and disappointment.

It is in those moments of great discouragement the devil worked his way in and filled my thoughts with doubt and I was tempted to believe a great lie. God could have prevented all of this, the enemy whispered in my ear. If God loves you, why did He allow this to happen to you? If I choose to give in to those negative emotions and believe those lies, I begin to feel a great separation from God. Chaos comes in to my mind bringing me sadness and heartache instead of joy and peace. If I do not stand against the pain and the lies they can lead to disastrous mindsets and a place of depression. I know. I've been there.

I don't belong in that place, no one does. Yet it is so easy to go there. People may fail us but God never does. And even when we fail God, He is still there to pick up every piece of our broken hearts and put us back together again. I have learned that when we hurt, God hurts.

> *It is because of the Lord's mercy and loving-kindness that we are not consumed, because His [tender] compassions fail not.* (Lamentations 3:22 AMP)

Chapter One

What I Didn't Expect When I was Expecting

For we do not have a High Priest Who is unable to understand and sympathize and have a shared feeling with our weaknesses and infirmities and liability to the assaults of temptation, but One Who has been tempted in every respect as we are, yet without sinning. (Hebrews 4:15 AMP)

I am a woman of convenience, a woman who will pay full price to have it yesterday. I am a woman who doesn't like to settle for anything less; when I want what I want, that's what I want. But God is not on the same page with me on that facet of my personality. I want to scream; "God, do you know how this feels? Do you know how hard this is? Do you know that I cannot take much more? Do you know that I could go crazy? Do you know this hurts?" Once I stop and get still before Him, His answer is always, YES! God does know how we hurt; He does know how we feel.

Daily, I am learning that patience produces in me the person that God wants me to become. Even when I cannot express it I have learned to just say, "God, You know me, You know how I feel and I need You. I need help." There are even some days I cannot muster the strength to get that far and I just say a simple, "Dear God…" and leave it at that. I believe that in its purest form that is my heart's cry; Dear God.

The Most Tragic and Beautiful Day of Our Lives

The reality of the rollercoaster of emotions and fears we have experienced in our life overwhelms me sometimes. I try to remember what it felt like when all was well. July 1, 2005, our baby boy was healthy and kicking me as we waited in great expectation for his arrival. We had carefully chosen his name, one with great meaning and honor to our faith and our family, Matthew Clark Weatherly. He was perfect.

July 2, 2005, was to be the most tragic and beautiful day of our lives. I shed tears of emotion even now as I relive the emotions of that day. We were overjoyed with our baby's impending arrival. We knew it would be that day when I began early signs of labor. We dressed; made sure our son Nathan was with his Nay Nay, my sister Lynette, and went to Lowe's to shop for the new home we were building. We had called the doctor to report my signs of labor and we were to meet him later that afternoon at the hospital. As this was our second child, we knew what to expect. We knew we had plenty of time to stroll through Lowe's planning for the new home we would bring our new baby home to. With beams of joy across our faces, we looked with great anticipation to this, Matthew's birth day!

We picked out porch lights for our home as we excitedly discussed what would go where in our beautiful new home. We still had plenty of time so we stopped for lunch and laughed almost all of the time we were so full of joy and excitement. My heart races as I remember how I felt at that moment. It was a moment of life and joy; a moment of great expectation. But it was the last time we would be like that with our son thriving inside of me, his heart beating strong, his legs letting me know it was time to meet us! When we checked into the hospital, I was only ½ centimeter dilated so we called our families who had already begun gathering for our annual Weatherly & Clark Fourth of July bash and told them it looked like Matthew's arrival was going to be delayed a while longer.

As they prepared to release me to go home, my water broke and labor went in to full swing. Our families quickly arrived at the hospital in anticipation of Matthew's arrival. My labor was more intense then I remembered from our first child and the pain was unbearable. This was not what I had expected. I knew something was seriously wrong. I began to go in and out of consciousness as I went through what should have been a normal vaginal delivery.

At 9:42 pm Matthew Clark Weatherly was born, at 10:07 pm he went to be with Jesus. My memory is vague on a lot of things that went on during those few hours. What I do remember has given me many nightmares over the years since that day. I remember him not crying. I remember pleading with someone to tell my why he was not crying. I could feel the deep concern all over the room. I remember the intense pain and screaming for relief and help. I remember an image of seeing his little feet lying on the table near my bed right before I was taken to what would be my first surgery of the night. Then there was the second surgery which resulted in an emergency hysterectomy. I was in critical condition, they weren't even sure if I would live.

The Unexpected

These moments in our lives hit hard. They are unplanned and unexpected. There is no time to evaluate how close we are to God. No time to reflect on those Sunday sermons or realign our spiritual ship. They come suddenly, in moments when our expectations are quite the opposite. It is in those moments of crisis that we react based on who and what we really are. Ronnie Weatherly

"Do whatever you have to do to save my wife," were words I never expected to say. I didn't expect to feel so helpless as I held my son, Nathan, not knowing if he would ever speak to his mommy again. I didn't expect to see the Red Cross doing a blood drive for my wife who was bleeding to death in the hospital delivery room behind us. I looked at the camera hanging around my neck. I expected to be taking pictures with our brand new healthy baby boy as Lori glowed with the look only new mamas possess. I expected to have two sons that would call me daddy and have a family of four to love and support.

As I sat there in the hallway with Nathan by my side, I looked into his eyes as I trembled at the very thought of his mother leaving us, just as Matthew had done just a while before this awful moment. Confused and afraid, I relied upon my faith and my family for support. As Lori was fighting for her life, Nathan and I were ushered into a small room where we could say our hellos and our good-byes to our little Matthew. We looked at one another not understanding what just happened. As I kissed Matthew good-bye, I fervently prayed we would not be saying good-bye to his mother.

In those hours that followed as we sat outside the Operating Room door, I found myself going from the Dad saying goodbye to his newborn son to the husband saying hold on to my wife, my best friend. As we watched the doctors and nurses go in and out of the Operating Room doors, I could see the concern and worry on their faces. There were no encouraging words or expressions to give; just somber looks of, "We're doing all we can." I held Nathan tight and in that moment he was my comfort as we prayed and pleaded with God to save his mother, my wife.

Parents Never Expect...

A lot of complications, death and despair enveloped our families as they dealt with Matthew's passing and me being in critical condition. Miraculously, two weeks to the day of being admitted into the hospital, I was released. I didn't know what had happened to me, I didn't understand it at all. When it was time to leave, my mom and Ronnie were with me, but not my baby. I started crying, and said to them "I just went in to have a baby." I expected to be returning home with him in my arms.

Instead, I left the hospital without him and in a much weakened fragile condition. It would be a long while before I understood how to process my grief and just how sick I really was. The physical trauma I had gone through was great, but my heart, my heart was so broken. No doctor, no pill could fix that. I had no idea at the time what the road to physical and mental recovery was going to be like for my husband and me. It was definitely not the road we expected to be on when we left the hospital that day.

Thursday, July 21, 2005, I awoke and told my husband, Ronnie I was ready to see a picture of Matthew. The only image I had of him was his two little feet. When Ronnie brought me the folder, I embraced it and cried as I opened it to see Matthew's beautiful face, his arms, his legs... his feet! He was so perfect. Tears streamed down my face. I couldn't understand how or why this happened. My finger traced over his precious little face on the pictures as I wept uncontrollably. I clung to those pictures as long as I had the strength to.

Parents never expect to have their children die before they do but on Saturday, July 23, 2005, we buried our little Matthew. I tremble as I think of my family and Ronnie walking and supporting me down the hallway at the funeral home. I told them couldn't do it. I couldn't go in there. I couldn't hold him. Leaning on Ronnie and mom for support, they stopped, let me breathe and told me, "Yes you can...

you have to." Then, as we rounded the corner of the room where his little white casket was, I couldn't get to him fast enough. I wept as I screamed for them to let me hold him. I have to hold him. I held him for two hours. I examined every little place on his body that I could. I whispered words in his ear that only he, God and I know. I told him how sorry I was that he couldn't be with us, but that he would always live in our hearts.

Death had truly gripped my heart. I wanted to die. I wanted to be with him. His little fingers were so purple, his lips as well. But he was perfect. He looked like me. During the viewing I held him and vaguely remember who was there, who I spoke to. I was never going to let him go, so I thought. Nathan, our five year old, kept covering his head because he said the baby was cold. He smiled at his brother and gave him a special car. He clung to our sides throughout the whole overwhelming experience. We buried Matthew with that special little car Nathan had placed between his tiny fingers.

For nine months I had waited in expectation, wondering how it would feel to hold the child that was growing within me. I expected to be Matthew's mama and in that moment, I was. I was Matthew's mama. I was holding my baby, and nothing else mattered. Ronnie came, put his arm around me and said, "Lori, it's time." I still remember it as if it was yesterday how I placed his cheek upon my cheek. He was so cold. I have chills just thinking of it. I close my eyes and go right back there and experience the smell of his face and the feel of his fingers. But as Ronnie gently lifted his little body out of my arms, I knew I had to let him go. Releasing Matthew's body would prove to teach me over time one of life's most valuable lessons... I would learn to love more deeply understanding that life is precious, moments in life are so worth having, and when you have the opportunity to make a memory, embrace it. That moment may have to last you a lifetime.

Matthew,

Once again your family has gathered together to share in thoughts of you.
It was just a few days ago that you came so quickly to us, but only stayed briefly. At that time we were gathered to welcome you, filled with thoughts of our beautiful baby boy and with anticipation to share in all the joys of a child's discoveries of life, love, family and friends.
Your Mother, who has so lovingly nurtured and sheltered you in her womb, awaiting the day that she could hold you, love you and protect you;
Your Father, who with pride announced your coming to everyone, looking forward to the days ahead when he could teach you, guide you and provide for all your needs;
Your big Brother, who has been filled with excitement at the thought of sharing all his childhood discoveries with you, anxiously ready to show you where all the frogs and lizards live;
And all your family: Grandparents, Aunts, Uncles, cousins and friends, expressing joy at the knowledge of your coming.
All of us looked forward to the days when we could share in your life and enjoy you being part of our lives.
*But YOU, Matthew, have made the greatest discovery of all......
The promise of the gift of eternal life.*

Our sadness and grief is for us to share because we miss you, but we can rejoice with you that your spirit is safe in God's love.

As we release these balloons, our messages of love are sent to you and we also remind ourselves, that just as these balloons rise one day we shall all rise to meet our Savior and share with you the greatest gift of all, eternal life with Jesus Christ.

Until we meet again, we will miss you and remember all the hopes and dreams of you.

We love you!

(This was written by my mother-in-law, Rose. She read it at Matthew's service just before we released balloons.)

 **Dealing with the Unexpected**

Grief brought my husband and me to a place we never expected to go. We did not have the slightest inclination that when we entered the hospital that day to deliver a healthy baby boy, we would come out dealing with not only his death but also the results of my physical trauma. We have had to learn to deal with the unexpected.

At the end of each chapter, we are going to share with you some of the lessons we have learned along the way in the hopes it will help you deal with the unexpected. Take the time to read through this section and allow God to minister to you. I would suggest you keep a journal and write down what you are feeling as you walk through this process with my husband and me.

There are two important lessons we learned as we began our journey back from the unexpected. First, in our weakness we must rely on HIS strength. In 2 Corinthians 12:8 Paul said, "Three times I pleaded with the Lord to take it (a thorn in the flesh) away from me." Like Paul, we pleaded with God to take our pain away. Paul shares what God told him in 2 Corinthians 12:9. "But he (the Lord) said to me, 'My grace is sufficient for you, for my power is made perfect in weakness.'"[1]

Are you facing a painful time in your life? _____ What does God say to us in 2 Corinthians 12:9? _____

Paul tells us how he dealt with unexpected hardships in verse 10. "That is why, for Christ's sake, I delight in weaknesses, in insults, in hardships, in persecutions, in difficulties. For when I am weak, then I am strong."[2] Explain what this means to you in your current hardship or painful situation: _____

The second thing we learned was time didn't and does not make it easier. It is God that gives us that innate ability to learn to cope through His word and His promises. Too many people put stock in "time" making it better and what we really need to trust in is God. God really does know how we hurt.

Read Hebrews 2:5-18 and realize that God knows the pain we are feeling. Jesus suffered everything we ever have and ever will suffer so that He could minister to us and bring us through to victory in Him.

> *For He did not subject to angels the world to come, concerning which we are speaking. But one has testified somewhere, saying, "What is man, that You remember him? Or the son of man, that You are concerned about him? You have made him for a little while lower than the angels; You have crowned him with glory and honor, And have appointed him over the works of Your hands; You have put all things in subjection under his feet." For in subjecting all things to him, He left nothing that is not subject to him. But now we do not yet see all things subjected to him. But we do see Him who was made for a little while lower than the angels, namely, Jesus, because of the suffering of death crowned*

---

[1] NIV
[2] NIV

with glory and honor, so that by the grace of God He might taste death for everyone.

For it was fitting for Him, for whom are all things, and through whom are all things, in bringing many sons to glory, to perfect the author of their salvation through sufferings. For both He who sanctifies and those who are sanctified are all from one Father; for which reason He is not ashamed to call them brethren, saying, "I will proclaim Your name to My brethren, In the midst of the congregation I will sing Your praise." And again, "I will put My trust in Him." And again, "Behold, I and the children whom God has given Me." Therefore, since the children share in flesh and blood, He Himself likewise also partook of the same, that through death He might render powerless him who had the power of death, that is, the devil, and might free those who through fear of death were subject to slavery all their lives. For assuredly He does not give help to angels, but He gives help to the descendant of Abraham. Therefore, He had to be made like His brethren in all things, so that He might become a merciful and faithful high priest in things pertaining to God, to make propitiation for the sins of the people. For since He Himself was tempted in that which He has suffered, He is able to come to the aid of those who are tempted. (NAS)

Thank you Heavenly Father that You are with us through the unexpected storms in our lives and that You love us and know the pain and weakness we feel. Thank You that in that weakness You are making us strong.

Chapter Two

An Unexpected Storm – Katrina

Then they cry to the Lord in their trouble, and He brings them out of their distresses. He hushes the storm to a calm and to a gentle whisper, so that the waves of the sea are still. (Psalm 107:28-29 AMP)

July 23, 2005, we buried our baby. August 29, 2005, Hurricane Katrina wrought havoc upon our lives and on those we love. We stayed in Pass Christian with my sister because I was still very sick, needed a lot of care and felt we needed to be near my doctors. I was scared to go anywhere. I was still very confused about what had taken place in my life and with Matthew.

Mom and the rest of our family were at her house just a few miles away. The last time I was able to contact my mother was in the early morning hours and as the storm approached I asked her, "Mom, are we going to die?"

She told me that she didn't know but she knew where to find strength to withstand the winds and rain of any storm. She told me to just quote scripture, so that's what I did through all the winds, the ripping off of the shingles, the trees, and the chaos of the storm. I sat with my nephews, my sisters and my son in a room waiting for what could have been the end of our lives here while our husbands took care of the house as things were being stripped away by the wrath of the hurricane.

The eye passed, and the calm came. My sisters each took an arm and walked me outside. The wind was still blowing and I was so weak I could not stand against the force of the wind. We walked through the debris and I had no thoughts of what I was experiencing. I felt like it was all a dream. I do know I was praying for the safety of those we loved.

Ronnie's mother was at a convention in Maryland. As she watched the devastation of the coast via media, she was overwhelmed by concern not knowing if we were even alive. Ronnie's dad and sister's family came the next day to locate us and make sure we were alright. My brother, Chuck, was in the hospital and had to be airlifted to Mobile due to the conditions of his health. He kept in touch as much as he could before we lost power. At one point he had paperclips chained all the way down his phone to get a signal from his room. He too, was watching the news wondering if we were all safe. It was literally a nightmare on top of another nightmare for all of our family members.

Ronnie and Todd left quickly after the storm and travelled through roads that were not safe to check on my parents and family members there. They had to get out of the truck to walk up the driveway due to the fallen trees surrounding their home. My mom said she was never so glad to see anyone in all her life. She knew then that all of her children were safe. Slowly, clearing debris, the men found their way to help others and find our families.

My brother's home was completely submerged under water. Eddie and his family lost all they had but they were safe. It was a heartbreaking scene everywhere we looked!

Everyone was alright physically, but most suffered extensive damage to their homes, property and land. Some of our friends did lose their lives, and some fought the waves clinging to any debris they could hold on to. When the unexpected storms of life hit, you begin to understand what is really important in life and where to put your faith and trust.

Our Lives, Our Economy, Our Businesses...Changed Forever

Reality set in. The coast as we knew it was changed forever as were our lives, our economy, and our businesses. Ronnie's business in Waveland was under nine feet of water. Just around the corner, my sister and I had a hair salon that had four feet of water. It was a roller coaster of emotions as we dealt with the loss of our son, my health and now, just five weeks after burying Matthew, the loss of our businesses.

The day Ronnie took me to see the salon for the first time, I went in expecting to feel a wave of emotion, but I was blank. I couldn't even cry. I just looked around in total disbelief as if what I was seeing had absolutely no emotional connection to me whatsoever. I wanted to feel anger and heartache over what we had worked so hard to build, but instead I stood in silence, feeling none of the above. We went to my husband's office and once again, the pile of debris seemed to me as just "stuff."

I was sorry for him, of course, but after experiencing the overwhelming loss of our son, looking at "stuff" that was destroyed by the hurricane just left me numb. I knew I should be feeling something at the loss of our belongings and our businesses, but I couldn't. As we drove down the beach and I saw all of the slabs that once were beautiful mansions, I felt nothing. What was wrong with me I wondered?

As we headed for where we had begun building our new home, I wondered what damage the hurricane had caused there. Surprisingly, only one shingle was bent with no other damage to our new home. As we walked up the driveway, there among the debris was this little orange and white note. It was wrinkled but had somehow survived the hurricane. I don't know whose house it blew out of, but it landed at mine and was a direct message from God for me. It had a scripture verse from Psalm 9:10 printed across the top. "Those who know your name will trust in you, for you, Lord, have never forsaken those that seek you."[3] I had never seen it before, but I sure needed to see it then. Out of all of the debris laying around our 3 acres... this little orange and white note was right in the middle... right where I would literally walk right over it! Amazing!

---

[3] NIV

We sent up a thank you prayer to our Heavenly Father for protecting our new home from the storm however the house we had been staying in during the building process was not so fortunate. A tree went through the roof of the kitchen upstairs. We were unable to return there so we lived with my parents until we could move into our new home.

Our New Home, Our New Life

Even as I was thanking God for protecting our new home in the storm, a new storm of grief washed over me as I remembered the day we found out we were expecting Matthew. We hurried home, pulled out the blueprints and immediately changed the guestroom into a nursery. We had been so excited! From that moment on, that was Matthew's room. The paint we had chosen for the nursery said Matthew's room; etched in my heart, Matthew's room. Nathan would proudly walk around the house as the walls went up and tell everyone his room was right next to his brother's, but he always added with a slight frown, they were going to have to share a bathroom.

After Matthew passed away, Ronnie had gotten behind on the building of our new home. A group of men from our church had organized a work day to pick up the slack knowing it would be difficult for Ronnie to take care of me and Nathan and work on the home. We were so touched and blessed by their acts of kindness. Now, just a few weeks later, many of those men needed help rebuilding their homes in the aftermath of Hurricane Katrina.

September and October were very rough months for everyone. It was a season of great recovery for everyone who lived along the coast but also of great change. Nothing would ever be the same again, for anyone who had lived through Katrina. For us, it meant another big change, Nathan was to begin kindergarten. I wasn't sure I could do it. I was scared to let him out of my sight. Thank God for his precious teacher Mrs. Tonya Perniciaro, who let me hide in her classroom closet crying while Nathan sat in class on the other side of the room. As I dealt with my own physical limitations, I suffered greatly with the insecurity of not being able to be a good mom in "my condition."

Determined to cover up my grief, I began teaching myself how to stay in complete composure when someone would ask how I was doing. An endless sea of doctor appointments was now my routine. Total dependence upon my family and my husband were how I had to survive so I wore the mask of composure until in the quietness of being by myself, I would give into the waves of grief and totally lose it.

One day as Ronnie and I were on our way home from the neurologist, we were in downtown Gulfport where we had lived for the months prior to the hurricane. I couldn't remember any street names, I couldn't recognize where we were. I was terrified! We were literally four blocks from where we used to live, yet I was lost, completely lost. I had many moments like that over the next few months; it was like I was watching a movie of some place I had never been and wondering what it all meant!

We moved into our not quite complete home in November of 2005. It would be months before it would be complete with countertops and cabinet doors, but we had a home which is more than a lot of our friends and neighbors had. We learned rapidly that things like missing countertops and cabinet doors really didn't matter. Whether I made coffee on the bathroom countertop or in the kitchen was no big deal. What filled my thoughts was the grim reality of not being able to fill the nursery with the hopes and dreams we had for the baby we had designed it for. I had envisioned two boys on one side of the house playing cars and throwing baseballs together, but instead there was only silence each time I entered Matthew's room.

As the deafening silence enveloped me, I grieved for the lack of laughter and the absence of peek-a-boos. There was crying, though, lots of crying, but it was not a baby's cry, it was a mother's anguished weeping. My tears soaked into the carpet as I pleaded with God to take this pain away. Though the four walls pierced my heart and stung my soul every time I entered the room, for some reason, once I entered I never wanted to leave it. When guests would come and tour our new home, I always said it was Matthew's room. I could not stand it when someone would call it any different. Storms of grief continued to wash over me as we strove to finish our new home, a home that was for three now instead of four.

Storms of Grief

I shut everyone out of my life except for our families. I wouldn't take calls even from some of my best friends. I couldn't bear to hear about the loss of their homes and the sadness that they had inside of them. Even though I was sad for them, I felt resentment because though they may not have had a bed to tuck their children in to at night, they had their children. I would have given all that I had for that.

As days went by, depression became my friend. My escape became shopping; shopping for anything. I would get a "high" off buying something new but when I got it home, the feeling was gone and I didn't want it any longer. Whatever I bought never brought me the peace and joy I so desperately needed and longed for in my heart.

Ronnie took me to Louisiana to shop for and order our living room furniture. It was fun picking it out and then the sales person told me it would take about 8 weeks to come in. During those next 8 weeks, I was in a state of great expectation. I kept imagining how it would make our home cozy and comfortable. In a moment of reflection, I realized the last time I expected something good was the day our son was born. It was almost euphoric in a sense to have that feeling of expectation again. Maybe I was actually getting better.

The day our furniture was delivered, I was so excited. I watched as the guys carefully put the entertainment center together and brought in the couch and each new cushion. I couldn't wait for them to leave so I could just relax on the couch and settle in. As I shut the door behind them, my heart sank. I sat on the floor and began to cry. The great expectation of joy was gone now that what I had been expecting had arrived. We had the furniture but I was still so sad. It didn't fix me. It only made me realize that I couldn't ever go back to that day, July 1st, 2005 when the nervous excitement and expectations were at their peak! It was an emotion I felt I could never attain again, no matter what I purchased. I was immediately reminded of the feelings I experienced on July 2nd after the unexpected happened. I sat there amidst my new furniture and relived the biggest let down of my life.

I knew I had a serious problem. I had no hope. I held my head high for everyone else, but inside I was dying. I entered every doctor appointment with great hope, only to leave with great disappointment and then an hour's worth of crying as we made our way home. Ronnie began to anticipate the let down and would insist on a trip to the mall where he knew for at least a few minutes I would have relief and escape the reality of what life was for us now. What neither of us realized at the time was that not only did we need to grieve, it was a necessary part of the healing process.

It Is Necessary to Grieve

It was during the next few months that I began to have increasingly negative and some times really awful thoughts. I would think about going to the hospital and taking the newborn babies away and then asking all of the mothers just how they felt. It was awful. I hated myself for having those thoughts. I couldn't look at baby boys. The girls didn't bother me, but the boys broke my heart. I would just see a blue baby blanket and want to die. Grief brought me to a place I had never expected to go. Because I didn't want anyone to know I was falling apart, I held it together. I felt as though I was expected to be "just fine." Everyone kept saying, "Time will heal…" But I didn't heal, I only got worse.

For some reason it became very important for me to keep up the appearance that I was just fine. Before tragedy, I was healthy, strong and energetic. I had a very successful career and was a very active mother and wife. After the injury, not only was my identity gone, I had lost my son so part of my family was gone as well. I hated life. I wanted to die. But I certainly couldn't let anyone know that. There was nothing a little lipstick and mascara couldn't cover or fix up for me. I maintained the outside while I was slowly eroding on the inside.

I felt somehow responsible for living up to the "standards" others had for me. In public, when I would run into someone who knew me before, they would say, "You look great! I am so glad you are doing good." I would smile and say, "Yes, I am, thank you." But on the inside I was saying, "Who me? Good? No, not at all!" I was hiding behind a mask of what I thought others expected of me while I protected myself from being hurt again. I didn't allow anyone into my space because I didn't trust them with what little I had left amid the ashes of what my life had been.

My identity was gone and so were the many hopes and dreams I had for Matthew's life, for my life, and for our lives as a family. In an instant, they were gone. The unexpected had stolen everything from me but I didn't want anyone to see me grieving the loss of my own son and the loss of my life as I knew it. Perhaps it was because the physical pain was so overwhelming that I felt as if I had to stay strong or I would crumble.

I never grieved over the loss of my son. I didn't know how to, nor did I have time to wallow in my grief. I had to fight just to live. I had to fight the biggest physical battle I had ever faced. I went from a healthy, vibrant successful business woman, wife and mother to a near invalid. I wish I would have felt safe enough to grieve. I wish I would have allowed myself to grieve. But instead I went into survival mode. I was a survivor of a tragedy; a survivor who had lost her son and now had to fight to live for her other son.

I didn't realize how much self-inflicted pressure I was putting on myself to wear that mask of, "I'm OK." I think I felt if I were down, I would be letting those I love down and then they would be sad for themselves and sad for me. The pressure to be "OK" was tremendous for me because, I was not "OK." Life was going on around me. I was jealous that there were mamas tucking all their babies in bed at night when one of mine was gone. How could people smile and laugh around me when I was living in a silent hell every single day?

Sometimes the anger would seep out like the day a diaper commercial came on TV and I screamed for someone to change the channel. I was so mad! Anger and confusion played a huge part of the hardening of my heart. Many days I had to fight with myself just to get out of bed, to function and go on with life when all I wanted to do was suffer silently, alone. It was almost as if as long as I was hurting inside emotionally, I would not forget Matthew. How could I smile when my son had died? Guilt began to eat away at me especially if I did happen to find a happy moment in some part of the day.

What Not to Say...

What I did learn during this time was what not to say to someone who is grieving for the loss of a loved one. I will never say to someone who is grieving, "All you need is time." I wish everyone who wanted to help me but were at a loss for words would have said nothing instead of that. Then there were those who said, "At least you have Nathan..." That would get me in the gut every time. I would think to myself as the anger welled up inside of me, "Let me take one of your kids and say, 'well at least you have one more,' and see how comforting that is for you." I learned so much about what NOT to say when someone is grieving.

I also learned everyone needs to grieve. And, most importantly, it is not just okay to grieve, it is necessary! I am still working through that part of the process and I am now allowing myself to experience grief. There is also not a time table for grieving. I think a lot of people think after a certain amount of time passes, grief also should pass. With God's help and my family's support, we are facing this and understanding God's purpose and His plan for our lives as it unfolds day to day.

Ronnie's Thoughts

You ever get the feeling that you just want to yell, "This isn't fair!" to God? Needless to say I didn't just feel it. As I watched Hurricane Katrina begin to strengthen into a full blown category four level storm, I thought about the past five weeks my family had been through. We had just buried our son, Lori's recovery was not going nearly as expected and we were terribly behind in building our new home, not to mention how things were piling up at work. It was supposed to have been our time of grieving and healing but there on the TV screen was Hurricane Katrina, heading right for us!

We are not given the promise of a perfect life. We live in a natural world and we are subject to those forces. The fact is God did not send that storm to destroy our businesses and friends' homes. It is simply the way God has designed our earth to cool itself. Much has been made concerning the trials we face in this world but the fact is we were never promised a life without trials. What we are promised is that God will be with us during these trials. It is in His presence that we find our hope and our strength.

It is in these moments I am reminded that it is not God's blessings we should be after but His presence. In Exodus Chapter 32, Moses was interceding for God's forgiveness after the Israelites built the golden calf and he lost his temper breaking the tablets containing the Ten Commandments. Then in Exodus Chapter 33, Moses demonstrates a truth which I have learned to hang on to. God promises Moses an angel to clear a path and go with them. God had given Moses His blessing but in Exodus 33:15 Moses says, "If your Presence does not go with us up from here, do not send us up from here."[4] Moses wanted more than just God's blessing, he wanted God's presence. He would refuse the blessing without God's presence.

After Katrina I saw so many people devastated by the loss of their blessings. I too was devastated. Matthew was a blessing, Lori's hair salon was a blessing, my business was a blessing, and Lori's health was a blessing. When all that was stripped away, God was still there. I have learned to pray that it is not God's blessing I seek but His presence. The distinguishing factor in my life is not the blessings. We are not characterized by our blessings. The distinguishing factor is God's presence.

I am reminded of a New Testament story about the Apostle Paul in Acts chapter 27. I was especially drawn to verse 17 which says, "Fearing that they would run aground on the sandbars of Syrtis, they lowered the sea anchor and let the ship be driven along."[5] I have read and heard many preachers talk about facing storms and being able to throw out anchors to stabilize the ship in life's great tempests. It was in my family's storm I threw out my anchor of hope. My hope was in God and knowing He was in control. I didn't understand how or why all of this was happening; I just knew He was my anchor in the storm. Most sermons I have heard have failed to discuss the importance of having those anchors in place **before you ever set sail**. I thank God for having had that anchor in place before we hit those unexpected storms. We do not know when those unexpected storms may hit, that is why we must carry our anchors with us every day.

---

[4] NIV

[5] NIV

This was so that, by two unchangeable things [His promise and His oath] in which it is impossible for God ever to prove false or deceive us, **we who have fled [to Him] for refuge might have mighty indwelling strength and strong encouragement to grasp and hold fast the hope appointed for us and set before [us]. [Now] we have this [hope] as a sure and steadfast anchor of the soul [it cannot slip and it cannot break down under whoever steps out upon it—a hope] that reaches farther and enters into [the very certainty of the Presence]** *within the veil.* (Hebrews 6:18-19 AMP emphasis added)

Dealing with the Unexpected

How do we get that anchor of hope Ronnie spoke about? If we don't expect something to happen in our lives, like the devastation caused by Hurricane Katrina, how can we be prepared enough to weather the storm?

Living on the coast of Mississippi and at sea level, the authorities were constantly warning us and instructing us to prepare ahead of time for the possibility of storms coming up unexpectedly and racing across the Gulf of Mexico to slam into our coast line. Those who follow this advice are much more likely to survive no matter when or where or how powerful the storm coming against them might be.

As Christians, we need to make sure we have adequately prepared for the unexpected storms of life just like those of us on the Mississippi coastline must always be prepared for the unexpected waves of destruction caused by hurricanes.

Easton's Bible Dictionary says this about an anchor: *In Hebrews 6:19 the word (anchor) is used metaphorically for that which supports or keeps one steadfast in the time of trial or of doubt. It is an* emblem of hope. "If you fear, put all your trust in God: that anchor holds."[6]

Read these scriptures on where you need to put your hope and trust so you will have your anchor of hope firmly secured when the unexpected storms of life come against you and your family. Underline the source of hope given in each verse.

Psalm 42:5 says, "Why are you downcast, O my soul? Why so disturbed within me? Put your hope in God, for I will yet praise him, my Saviour and my God" (NIV).

Psalm 62:5-6 says, "Find rest, O my soul, in God alone; my hope comes from him. He alone is my rock and my salvation; he is my fortress, I will not be shaken" (NIV).

Psalm 147:11 says, "The Lord takes pleasure in those who reverently and worshipfully fear Him, in those who hope in His mercy and loving-kindness" (AMP).

Isaiah 40:31 gives us an amazing promise if we put our hope in Him. Underline that promise. "But those who wait for the Lord [who expect, look for, and hope in Him] shall change and renew their strength and power; they shall lift their wings and mount up [close to God] as eagles [mount up to the sun]; they shall run and not be weary, they shall walk and not faint or become tired" (AMP).

Now read Hebrews 6:18-19 and personalize it as your "anchor of hope" by writing your name and your family's names in the blanks.

This was so that, by two unchangeable things [His promise and His oath] in which it is impossible for God ever to prove false or deceive us, we (_____) who have fled [to Him] for refuge might have mighty indwelling strength and strong encouragement to grasp and hold fast the hope appointed for us (_____) and set before [us]. [Now] we (_____

---

[6] Easton, M. 1996, c1897. *Easton's Bible dictionary.* Logos Research Systems, Inc.: Oak Harbor, WA

_____) have this [hope] as a sure and steadfast anchor of the soul [it cannot slip and it cannot break down under whoever steps out upon it—a hope] that reaches farther and enters into [the very certainty of the Presence] within the veil. (Hebrews 6:18-19 AMP emphasis added)

Chapter Three

The Unexpected Emotions of First Holidays

~~~

Everyone is singing ..."Give thanks with a grateful heart, give thanks to the Holy One, give thanks because He's given Jesus Christ His Son... and now, let the weak say I am strong, let the poor say I am rich, because of what the Lord has done for us... give thanks."

November 20, 2005

Dear Friends and Family,

As the holiday season is here, we have so much to be thankful for. In lieu of the traditional cards we send, we decided tis' the season for a letter of thanksgiving from our family. The year of 2005 has brought many changes in our lives. It began with the news of expecting a baby as we were building a new house. From that point, we began to build not only our new home, but also hopes and dreams for our expanding family. We soon realized how quickly life can change. On July 2, we had a beautiful baby boy, Matthew Clark Weatherly, 8 lbs, 14 oz and 22 inches long. He came into the world at 9:42 pm and was placed in the arms of Jesus at 10:07 pm. As we are trying to heal emotionally, Lori is still recovering physically as doctors and therapists work to correct the injuries sustained during that time.

We have since then moved into our new home. Nathan is still a wonderful big brother and we are the proud parents of two beautiful boys... Matthew just has a different address. We are comforted in knowing our mail will forward there one day as well. Nathan is enjoying kindergarten and learning to read. His new best friend is our four month old Weimaraner, Dixie. Our cat, Lily, has welcomed Dixie with open paws and claws. One of the three is always into something.

Hurricane Katrina flooded both of our businesses and affected many of our friends and families' lives. Once again, we realize the importance of praying and supporting each other as we all rebuild our lives.

We thank you all so much for the love, support and prayers that have been extended over the past five months. We are looking ahead as we believe God is not finished yet with the miracle He has begun. As we started the year we had many great expectations... as we close the year, we count our many blessings.

Happy Thanksgiving,
Ronnie, Lori and Nathan

May God give you peace, joy, and an abundance of love as we have many reasons for this season to be the best of them all.

Thanksgiving 2005

Thanksgiving is a time to reflect upon our blessings and to be thankful for everything. It seems like it should be a challenge considering what we have weathered the past few months, however, I feel an overwhelming sense of gratitude more now than ever. I also feel an overwhelming sadness without Matthew, a sadness that is depleting me of all the energy and strength I have left. I really do not understand how I can feel so grateful and sad at the same time. I really can't comprehend how I can be so angry and in the same breath offer up a prayer of thanksgiving. But the truth is that seems to be the course of my emotions these days.

I know God's Word says in everything give thanks and I so want to do that. So as my tears flow out of my eyes and my heart is filled with the pain of grief, I thank God for eyes that can cry and a heart that can feel. But I wish I didn't feel so sad, so scared and so hurt. I am sad that my baby isn't here with us. My heart hurts and my tears sting as the festivities begin to gain momentum all around me. I wish I could just skip over all of this; all of the holidays. My throat closes up as if to strangle me as I think of Thanksgiving, Christmas, Easter, and his first birthday. I just want to take a pill and sleep through the next seven months.

I want to survive but with all these first holidays so rapidly approaching, I don't know if I can live through all the ups and downs and unexpected conflicting emotions. I thought the roller coaster of emotions was bad before, now they are nearly unbearable. I just want the hurt to go away. Everyone is singing ..."Give thanks with a grateful heart, give thanks to the Holy One, give thanks because he's given Jesus Christ his son... and now, let the weak say I am strong, let the poor say I am rich, because of what the Lord has done for us... give thanks."

    I am weak Lord... very weak.
        I am thankful Lord... very thankful.
            I am scared Lord... very scared and I need you.
                I don't want turkey, holiday cheer or presents.
                I want my son.

The Therapy of Journaling

On November 28, 2005, I began a very important part of my healing process. I began to journal my feelings and my thoughts. I had therapy today. My strength is improving, but I have to work more on balance. Therapy is very frustrating to me but it also makes me appreciate all of the things I used to be able to do. I am actually feeling okay on the inside. I am trying to stay on the up as I focus on things to be thankful for. There are moments I have to just be thankful I am alive so I can keep my sanity.

A dear friend recommended that as I start my journaling to read Jeremiah Chapter 1 and Ecclesiastes Chapter 3. Ecclesiastes 3:1-15 particularly impacted me as I faced the upcoming holiday season. I underlined and highlighted it so it would be forever stamped in my mind. I thought to myself, Solomon must have experienced the same wide range of conflicting emotions I am to have written such powerful words.

> *There is a time for everything, and a season for every activity under heaven: a time to be born and a time to die, a time to plant and a time to uproot, a time to kill and a time to heal, a time to tear down and a time to build, <u>a time to weep and a time to laugh, a time to mourn and a time to dance</u>, a time to scatter stones and a time to gather them, a time to embrace and a time to refrain, a time to search and a time to give up, a time to keep and a time to throw away, a time to tear and a time to mend, a time to be silent and a time to speak, a time to love and a time to hate, a time for war and a time for peace. What does the worker gain from his toil? I have seen the burden God has laid on men. He has made everything beautiful in its time. He has also set eternity in the hearts of men; yet they cannot fathom what God has done from beginning to end. I know that there is nothing better for men than to be happy and do good while they live. That everyone may eat and drink, and find satisfaction in all his toil--this is the gift of God. I know that everything God does will endure forever; nothing can be added to it and nothing taken from it. God does it so that men will revere him. Whatever is has already been, and what will be has been before; and God will call the past to account.*

It is amazing how being truly thankful at all costs can change one's heart. I have gotten a lot of responses from the Thanksgiving newsletter I wrote sharing my feelings on being thankful. No matter what my mood, or how down I am, I am really trying my best to focus on our blessings. Now I just need to keep taking my own advice and make this my new life style. I need to settle in to the new me.

The New Me

December 2, 2005. Five months today. I wonder when I will stop doing that; thinking it's been one month, two months, three then four and now five months since that day. It seems like yesterday in so many ways but then so much has happened since then that sometimes I have trouble focusing in on the present. Many memories are coming to my mind as Ronnie and I reflect on those weeks when I was in the hospital. It's such a scary time for me to remember. Every time we try to go back and sort out it all out, the horrible memories begin to surface and then the flashbacks flow in waves as they haunt my mind and play over and over and over. How can anyone understand what it felt like to be so helpless, to know I was dying yet not really know what was going on? Some memories are so vivid, while many other moments I do not seem to be able to remember at all.

What I do remember is the fear. It grips me again and threatens to suffocate me. Then the anger tries to overcome my happiness and gratefulness to be alive. I hope I outgrow the way I feel. I don't want to be bitter or angry. I am so blessed to be alive; I have to pray this through. Grief is so overwhelming at times that I can't seem to look beyond it. I am trying so hard to "like" the "new me." I know I am never going to be like I was before but I still try to see some resemblance of myself when I look in the mirror. The trouble is that person is not there any more. Nothing is or will ever be the same again. My heart is broken. I miss my baby terribly and I miss myself, the energetic healthy person I was before. How do I truly embrace this new me when every time I look at her I remember what I've lost?

December 3, 2005, a new day dawns but the waves of depression have not subsided. Today was very hard, almost unbearable and I was angry at everything or everybody. I do not know how to explain my feelings. I've never been so emotional, I cannot control myself. I am angry and frustrated with this new me. My body is a mess. My hair is falling out and my feet are slowly deforming; not to mention all of the bad stuff in between! I've got to figure out a way to live again. I want to laugh again, but I can't. I want to cry but I feel like I have to stay strong for everyone so they will think I am okay and not worry about me. But the trouble is, "I'm NOT OK!" I just want to scream at the world from the top of my lungs, "This is hard and it isn't getting any easier!"

As I cry out to God in my frustration and my pain, He shows me a picture that calms my heart and stills my raging emotions. I see Matthew in His arms. I believe He is holding my special little boy right now and that He will restore our empty arms and heal my broken heart. What a sweet moment it will be when Jesus hands me my little boy. I long to feel his soft face again on my cheek and to hold his hand again. I'll never ever forget holding him though the moment was so very brief. God please give that back to me. Only You can fill the vacancy I feel in my life. Our lives are in Your hands. You know my heart, my intentions and my prayer and I know that You will not fail me. Heal my body and my broken spirit; renew my life so that I may live again. Help this new me to become what You want me to be!

Christmas, A Time Of Miracles

As we approached the Christmas season, I felt useless, worthless and embarrassed at what had become of me physically. I had begun to pray daily for healing and restoration. As I did I began to receive cards from the thousands of people all over the country that had me on their prayer lists. It was quite overwhelming to read the hundreds of cards sent and the support and encouragement from hundreds of people that came to my family in that tragic time. I will never underestimate the power of prayer or the need for prayer. I don't just believe in miracles, I depend upon them!

December 7, 2005 was not a particularly good day. I saw a Physical Therapist today and my pelvic exam was not so great. On a scale of 1-5 with 5 being best, I scored a 1-2. I feel nothing but a little pressure in the lower parts of my body. I asked the therapist if she had ever had a patient in my condition and her answer was like all of the rest of the specialists I had seen. She had never worked with someone with total sensory loss such as I had. When I left the room, she told my mother-in-law Rose, that she and her baby had survived having a uterine rupture. I wanted to know why I didn't have my baby and why I was not well and working like she was. Matthew was perfect; I screamed to myself, he shouldn't have died!

I kept having these fits of anger. When I got home that day from the therapy, I sat and watched Nathan playing and realized my up and down emotions were stressing him out as well. He had lost 8 pounds since November 10th. I needed to pull myself together and deal with this Christmas season for Nathan and Ronnie. I started praying and later sat and talked with Ronnie about what we should do to help Nathan. We agreed we needed a miracle and prayed together against the anger I was feeling and for our Nathan.

We knew we needed help for Nathan and my friend Tina was able to step in and talk with Nathan and with me. She helped us to try and understand the stages of grief and aided us tremendously in our journey of figuring things out. Her professional help was really appreciated, most importantly though she was a praying friend who encouraged me many days and prayed for me and my family without hesitation. We were so thankful for her help and comfort during a very stressful time.

As I awoke on December 11, 2005, my thoughts turned to Matthew. Then I heard the sounds of my family moving around and thought how thankful I was to be here with Ronnie and Nate on Christmas. I thanked God they were not facing a Christmas without me. They were already so sad that we were without Matthew. My hair is falling out by the handfuls and I look awful. From my head to my toes I am physically a wreck, however I am doing my best to recover and be strong. I slap my wig on, put on some lipstick and a smile. I still struggle daily as I look in the mirror at this new me but I vow to remain thankful as I face what each day brings.

December 12, 2005, was another trip to the Physical Therapist. I came out with less then encouraging news, again. My biofeedback test was only .09- the rest stage is .03 ☹. My therapist would like me to be a 10! She could even not find a 'flick' of feeling until she examined my pelvic muscles while doing the procedure. All the more reason, I thought, that when God heals me they will know without a shadow of a doubt that it was Him and nothing they did. I believe God will heal me and these specialists will know only God could have fixed my broken body. My God is a God of miracles. Just look at what He did at Christmas! His only Son was born of virgin mother, wrapped in an old blanket and laid in a stable of all places!

I awoke on December 13. 2005, still basking in the blanket of God's love. I thanked Him for the healing He was bringing me and all of a sudden, I got the feeling back in my big toe on my left foot!!! It was so weird – I could not stop touching it! God works in mysterious ways, I thought! He has started my healing with my big toe! Hope is what this brings to me as I realize what an awesome God we have! A tiny miracle but a miracle nonetheless! I knew I would recover sensory feeling; He gave me that precious hope!

Ronnie and I also talked about my writing career today. I told him how I felt and he is very supportive. He read what I had already written and we are very comfortable in this decision. For the first time, I sense the purpose of all of this. We know what direction to go. Suddenly I felt a peace I have not had in a long time. Another miracle, two in one day!

I almost looked forward to therapy today, December 14, 2005. I couldn't wait to show off my big toe! Therapy was hard and my left leg was still very weak but I felt pain in my big toe! As a matter of fact it was very sore, although I will not complain about the pain. My therapist said the toes are usually the last thing to get feeling back after such a trauma. Of course, I thought to myself, God would make me an exception to medical books! He just wants to keep them guessing and show them all He is the miracle maker!

After therapy we went to see Matthew's monument. They were to have set it in place today. We were not happy with the picture or the base but they will fix it and it was nice to see something out there for him. We took some Christmas decorations with us and I planted a little Christmas tree there for him. Nathan sat upon the side of his brother's tombstone so I could take a picture of what should have been both of my healthy boys by our Christmas tree inside our home. I am so sorry he is not here with us. I miss him so much and I want his monument to be perfect. It's not there yet, but it will be. Just like me. God is still working on me. I am not perfect yet but I will be!

It is December 16, 2005, and mom and I decided to go Christmas shopping. I fell yesterday so I wasn't feeling too well to start with. I woke this morning with a lot of back pain and it was midday before it began to loosen up. I wasn't really in the mood to purchase presents but then I thought how really grateful I was to be here for this Christmas. When I told Nathan we were going Christmas shopping today, his eyes just lit up and that made it all worth it! I had been so close to death, that just thinking I might not have been here for him freaks me out. I am so thankful I get to be here with Ronnie, Nate and our families. God's great love and mercy has preserved my life and now He is showing me why.

I spent the first part of the day on December 20, 2005, dealing with cabinet stuff, again. I am so ready to never deal with the stress of building a home ever again. Then I went to Nate's school for their Christmas program and party. He was singing Christmas carols and his face lit up when he saw me come in. I'm so thankful I could be there today. There are still many things stressing me out but I can say I have come a long way- thanks to God! I am learning to let the stress go. God did not fail us yesterday or today nor will He tomorrow. I expected to be sad this Christmas, and I was. But I didn't expect I could be thankful, but I am! Thank you God for the miracle of Your Son and for Your grace that has allowed me to be here with Nathan and Ronnie.

A New Year Dawns Bringing New Unexpected Emotions

I did pretty well until January 1, 2006. I looked at the calendar and the old thoughts surfaced once again. It will be six months tomorrow, I thought, I miss you terribly my baby! As grief began to fill my heart I thought, thank God the worst year of my life is over! Then the memories flooded in bringing with them a wave of guilt like I had never experienced before in my life!

Like a slap in the face, I realized I had not been able to protect my baby. My heart began to break as guilt stabbed me again and again. I was his mother, how could I not have known he was fighting for his life? I tried to imagine what it must have been like for him as he struggled for life that day. Did he wonder why I wasn't doing something for him? My heart grieved as I remember the first time I saw him was the Thursday before his service. I was sitting on the bed and asked Ronnie to show me what our boy looked like. The photo had broken my heart and as I looked at it again, I could see distress on his face. His forehead was white; it was just awful. He would have been 19 days old the day I looked at his picture for the very first time. Ronnie couldn't protect him, I couldn't protect him. He had needed us and we couldn't save him! To know he needed help that we couldn't give him is something we will never forget and never want to experience again.

For several months I silently battled the guilt. Why hadn't I known? Why hadn't I been able to do something? Why had I not been able to protect the little life that was within me? On April 27, 2006, I had a serious breakdown. I finally just screamed, "This is too hard!" It's hard to even write the words because they just aren't good enough to express what I was feeling. I am so tired of being sick. I want to be well now! I miss life so much. I miss Matthew more than ever. I am so sick of people telling me "time, all you need is time." Time will not bring my baby back to me.

On top of the guilt I felt for not being able to protect my baby, I thought about all I had put Ronnie through. I felt guilty that he had to live with me the way I am. I love him so much and want him to be happy but I can't even keep my own head above water, how can I make my husband happy? And what kind of a mother was I being to Nathan?

Ronnie pulled me close that night and we had a long talk. I am absolutely sure no other man could have been as supportive, loving and caring as he has been to me through all we have gone through. The pressure he feels has to be totally overwhelming for him, but at the end of each day he is there to hold me and say we made it. God, thank You for the man of strength and love You have given me. Hold my husband up in Your strong hand, Father until I can again be his helpmate.

Easter 2006

As I was getting ready for church Easter morning, my fingers grabbed the dress I had worn just a year before. It was the perfect Easter dress that I searched for hours for that would fit over my expanding belly as Matthew was taking occupancy within me. I wept as I remembered that most special Easter. We took family pictures. In one photo Nathan's head was laying on my stomach waiting for his brother to kick. Easter is always extra special for Nathan; he was born on Easter Sunday. Life was given to us as a family for the first time on Resurrection day! How awesome it was and I was expecting another new life to join us in just a few short months. I felt even more beautiful than I did on my wedding day. It was life within that was so beautiful, and I would never be that way again.

Easter Sunday of 2006 would be the first time I was able to go back to church. We found a church very close to home just in case I needed to leave in a hurry due to the many medical problems I was battling. When we walked into church, I felt so peaceful. I was so thankful to be back in church. I looked at Nate in his Easter Sunday best, smiling as he admired his new surroundings and Ronnie squeezed my hands as worship began. This was good. This was where we needed to be, in church, together.

After service, we went to the cemetery and Nathan decorated Matthew's grave with some very special eggs. It was a tender moment, but one that was filled with the promise of tomorrow. There were some tears, but also some smiles as we watched Nathan and his cousin Brett hide Easter eggs and enjoy the moment together.

Getting Out of the Corner

As I was praying early on April 29, 2006, I asked God if He had noticed that we have been faithful through all the unexpected events of the past year. I've never doubted Him and my faith has never waivered that God will restore what we lost- all of it. I also believe that does not mean it is easy to bear the loss and be patient as we wait to receive His promised restoration. It has been and still is incredibly hard. There are days I am in so much pain I just want to give up. I get so tired and my heart is broken but I know without a doubt that God is and always will be there. I went to church that night and the preacher looked me in the eyes and told me that God had seen my faithfulness and He was pleased. My time is not coming, the pastor said, it is now. His message to us that night was on the Book of Ruth, Chapters 1 and 2.

The message was "Getting Out of the Corner." When the preacher said, "Enough is enough, I am coming out of the corner," I knew God had a message for me. He told the story of a grieving mother named, Naomi and her newly widowed daughter-in-law, Ruth. Naomi was going to return to her own land after losing everything and told Ruth she had nothing to offer her and she should leave her and make a new life for herself.

Naomi quickly saw that Ruth was not leaving and would remain faithful to her promise in Ruth 1:16. "Where you go, I will go, and where you stay, I will stay. Your people will be my people, and your God, my God." Ronnie and I had spoken those very words to each other during our wedding ceremony; words that remain forever etched once spoken.

The preacher went on to say that Ruth had three marks against her; she was a woman, a Moabite and a widow. However, she was faithful and God honored her faithfulness by giving her favor through Boaz. Jesus is our Boaz, and that favor He gives us is His special approval. The preacher said we were to be like Ruth and "leave our familiarity alone and step out of the corner. God's favor always moves us forward."

This message really hit me because I had been in the corner for almost a year now, and would only surround myself with 'familiar' places, things and people. I was too scared to move forward. The preacher warned us, "When we are reminded of our past, it hinders our future." To me, that was just yesterday. I was afraid to move forward for fear what had happened physically to me yesterday would happen again tomorrow and the next day and the day after that.

It was time to get out of the corner and I knew that without moving forward, I would stay in the corner the rest of my life; afraid and trapped by my own fear. It was up to me, it was time to act upon my faith and trust that God would honor our faithfulness. My prayer earlier that day was asking God if He had seen that we had been faithful. His answer was, "Yes!"

And Jesus, replying, said to them, "Have faith in God [constantly]." (Mark 11:22 AMP)

May 14, 2006 - A Bittersweet Mother's Day.

Our pastor and his wife gave me a mustard seed pendant. I sure needed to be reminded of my faith, especially on this day. We went to the cemetery today and as we were leaving, Nathan said he would like to talk about how Matthew died and get a bench for the cemetery and discuss it sitting down. Ronnie and I looked at each other in surprise; however, I was not in an emotional state to handle that question at that moment. We said we would get a bench for the cemetery and Nathan dropped the subject. We went on with our day but later that night he asked again if we could discuss how Matthew died. I still wasn't sure I was prepared for what might be said but it turned out to be the sweetest story I have ever heard.

Ronnie sat down next to Nathan and said that mommy was losing all of her blood that day. "Matthew," Ronnie continued, "wanted mommy to live and be here with you and me, so he gave your mommy all of his blood so she could be here for us."

Nathan responded that he loved Matthew so much for doing that for him and his eyes were in awe of his baby brother giving up his life so I could live. My eyes were filled with tears, as were Ronnie's. We then realized that was exactly what had happened. How much he touched our lives all over again on that special moment on Mother's Day. You know God did that for us. He sacrificed His son so we could have eternal life with Him. Matthew's there already. As Ronnie says, "Matthew won the prize!" I am blessed to be the mother of two beautiful boys!

For truly I say to you, if you have faith [that is living] like a grain of mustard seed, you can say to this mountain, Move from here to yonder place, and it will move; and nothing will be impossible to you. (Matthew 17:20 AMP)

Dealing with the Unexpected

Any one who has ever lost a loved one will tell you the first set of holidays after their death are emotionally difficult to handle. The problem is no two people handle these unexpected emotions the same way. There is only One who can help any of us deal with the unexpected and the unexplainable. God is our source of peace and rest.

No matter what your loss, these scriptures from the heart of God will not only comfort you but give you what you need to live again. God, Himself suffered through the death of His own Son yet He willingly made that sacrifice that we may live in Him.

Read the following scriptures and begin journaling what the Lord is speaking to you in each one.

John 3:16 - *For God so greatly loved and dearly prized the world that He [even] gave up His only begotten (unique) Son, so that whoever believes in (trusts in, clings to, relies on) Him shall not perish (come to destruction, be lost) but have eternal (everlasting) life.* (AMP) _____

Matthew 11:28-29 -*Come to Me, all you who labor and are heavy-laden and overburdened, and I will cause you to rest. [I will ease and relieve and refresh your souls.]Take My yoke upon you and learn of Me, for I am gentle (meek) and humble (lowly) in heart, and you will find rest (relief and ease and refreshment and recreation and blessed quiet) for your souls.* (AMP) _____

John 14:27 - *Peace I leave with you; My [own] peace I now give and bequeath to you. Not as the world gives do I give to you. Do not let your hearts be troubled, neither let them be afraid. [Stop allowing yourselves to be agitated and disturbed; and do not permit yourselves to be fearful and intimidated and cowardly and unsettled.]* (AMP)_____

Chapter Four

Unexpected Revelation

On June 3, 2006, I journal the words Nathan said over dinner tonight, "Mama, I'm not glad that Matthew died." Nathan speaks of Matthew every day and we see that he too is dealing with a wide range of emotions just as we are. Again we realize it has not just been our loss of a son, Nathan also lost his brother. We told him that we were not glad either and that sometimes life doesn't seem right or fair.

My heart is pierced again as Nathan so sweetly concluded the conversation by saying, "I'll always love him and have him in my heart." Nathan speaks so tenderly when he refers to Matthew and has shown us repeatedly that he loves him as much as we do; his eyes literally light up at the mention of Matthew's name. Those sweet words come out of his mouth straight from his heart. I feel so protective of him, as does Ronnie. We grieve that we can't protect our living son from the disappointments of life any more than we were able to protect little Matthew that day in the hospital.

Disappointments, Nightmares and Memories

Life has seemed so full of disappointments, and to tell the truth, we are sick of them. So many days I want to quit. As July draws near, I feel depression coming over me and all I want to do is sleep, even though I never really sleep. The nightmares come on a regular basis now as we approach Matthew's first birthday. Once again I find that time has not helped me to "get over my loss" as so many people have tried to comfort me by saying. Not a day or a second goes by that I don't ache for my baby. Sometimes I have to remind myself to breathe and sometimes I don't want to take that breath. Then I think of Nathan and Ronnie, I never want to leave them. It is all so physically and emotionally painful; the nightmares, the memories, the smell of the hospital, then leaving the hospital without my baby. As I battle these emotions I find I cannot sleep.

Once again memory takes me back to the day of his birth and the overwhelming disappointment of the unexpected turn of events of that day. Then my mind swiftly takes me to the day of Matthew's service, the first time I saw him. I remember how I held him to my chest, how I felt his cheek next to mine and the embrace that lasted only a moment that I would never have again. That was the most beautiful as well as the most heartbreaking day in my life. Everyday I close my eyes and just ask Jesus to never, never, never let me forget the feel of his perfect little cheek touching mine. Oh, God, I miss that! I have slept with his blue bear every night since I came home from the hospital. I put it to my cheek and just cry. So many emotions are surfacing I feel as though I am suffocating beneath the weight of them. I can't sleep as the waves of emotion roll over me again and again.

Ronnie and I have spoken many times with Nathan about letting his bad memories go and replacing them with good ones. I so wish I could take my own advice and let go of those bad memories but the image of my beautiful baby is in the midst of all those memories. It's all we have, his memory. I will cherish that forever and never let it go though I do pray the nightmares and the torment would subside. It's been almost one year of torture, not only on my body, but on my heart. I know God will get us through it but so many days of anxiety and stress have worn me out! I need some peaceful, restful sleep!

"I just want something back!" I silently scream into my pillow, "If I can't have my baby, can't I at least have my health back?" I see people walking all around me and I miss being able to walk without being uncomfortable or limping. One thing I am sure to do everyday is have hope; without hope, I wouldn't want to be here. Each day is a choice and by God's grace we make it through to the next and the next.

This is the ad we placed in our local newspaper to honor Matthew on his first birthday, July 2, 2006:

Matthew Clark Weatherly
July 2, 2005

Each day we miss you so much. Each day we cherish you more...
every moment you were with us, every kick, every heartbeat.
We held you so close in hopes that feeling would never go away.
Your memory is always present in our heart and home.
Your big brother is crazy about you and can't wait to get to heaven
with you so he can show you where all the frogs are.

You came into our lives and it wasn't long enough. It's all we have and we are better than we ever were before because we love you and because God blessed us with being your family.
You changed our lives forever. You have the very best we could have given you… "You just have heaven before we do."
Happy 1st Birthday to our precious little boy!
We love and miss you so much.
Love, Daddy, Mommy, Nathan and your great big family
1 Samuel 1:27-28 "I prayed for this child, and the Lord has granted me what I asked of Him. So now I give him to the Lord."

July 25, 2006, just two days after the anniversary of Matthew's service, we returned home from our appointment with the neurologist with a less than encouraging report.

My neurologist said that I was young, motivated and energetic and that I had that going for me. But, that's all he could say. As Ronnie said on the way home, we needed the only doctor that had hope to doubt and now it's happened. Now God can heal me and no earthly physician can take any credit for it. I am so ready!

Turning Point

On July 26, 2006, I had the blessing of hearing a televised sermon by David Jeremiah that I believe was a turning point in my struggle for peace concerning the death of our dear Matthew. After the broadcast, I immediately wrote this letter to Dr. Jeremiah.

Dr. Jeremiah,

In the month of July, I had the blessing of hearing your sermon about children going to heaven and because our son passed away one year ago, your words spoke such peace into the depth of my soul. The reason I am writing you is to say "Thank You!" I received a personal letter from you as well and once again, your words were comfort to the both of us. Your letter was unexpected, yet greatly appreciated, and we still have days when we need reassurance from God that He's listening, and that was one of them. My dad has a phrase that "If God fails me this time, it will be the first time!" And through it all, God has never failed, and He is always on time, and so your letter was too! See, God is good!!!!

I would like to take a moment and share our testimony with you about the birth and death of our son. On July 2, 2005, I went into labor and while delivering our baby boy, I had a uterine tear. Due to the uterine tear, Matthew died just 25 minutes after he was born. I was in and out of consciousness and still bleeding to death. I had natural child birth and 2 surgeries within 6 hours. I was given a blood transfusion during the hysterectomy and went into renal failure as well, I flat lined twice. I remained on life support for 4 days, I had a NG tube, kidney stints, JP tubes, IV's, a pic-line and more. If there was a place for a needle or tube, I had it. I was very sick and had MANY complications.

The doctors (I had many of them!) all predicted I would be in the hospital 2-6 months, paralyzed, brain-damaged, or something like that.... I was discharged after 14 days (8 of those days in ICU.) I am NOT BRAIN-DAMAGED, NOT PARALYZED, and I did NOT have to have dialysis for my kidneys! I did leave the hospital very sick physically, and facing the ultimate heartbreak without my baby. I was so confused and on so many medications. I suffered extensive nerve damage to my buttocks, bowel and bladder, and the backs of my feet and legs. When I left the hospital I had yeast infections from antibiotics to my knees, internally I was a mess. I could not feel my legs, buttocks or bowel/bladder. I was a MIRACLE to be living, yet a MESS for God to finish me up. Each day was a chore to learn to walk.

Matthew was born on July 2; my 31st birthday was July 3. On July 23, 2005, I saw my baby for the first time, I held him, kissed him, loved him and let him go all in one day, the day we buried him. He was absolutely beautiful and PERFECT and ALWAYS will be with Jesus! I cannot begin to tell you of the road that we have traveled, but Jesus never left us! Five weeks after Matthew's funeral, Hurricane Katrina introduced herself to our area! We were safe, our families were safe, my brother with five children lost his house, *my husband and I both lost our businesses. The "aftermath" was incredibly hard, so many friends lost everything they had, sadness all around, depression, broken lives everywhere you looked!*

I had to lean on Jesus for strength and courage to fight. I was losing the battle fast. We did not have electricity for weeks, and I was still very infected, it was hot, only one cold shower a day, no bowel and bladder control...I hated living and I felt like a burden to everyone. But I wasn't. My husband loved me through it all, my family supported me through it all and Jesus never left me through it all. I am amazed at where I was physically at the time of the hurricane and where I am now.

Physically now, after a year of hard therapy, I walk good, exercise daily, I still do not feel the back of my legs, buttocks, bowel or bladder, I am at the doctor once a month for a check up. The doctors said that I probably will not get any feeling back since it is over the year mark. Actually, they are pretty pessimistic, but I BELIEVE God is in control, not them. I know God did not take my life for many reasons and I am not giving up. I want God to heal me and prove all of them wrong. This past week, I was able to walk across the house on my tip toes! (I have tried every day in therapy to stand on my toes and have not been able to on my left foot.) When I walked on them I was so excited and knew God was not done yet! The doctor never thought that was possible...But I expect it!!! I go to the doctor this week and can't wait to show him my new trick!

We have a 6 year old son that can't wait to be a big brother... again. We are in the process of adoption paperwork to make that happen. We are thrilled at the thought of bringing another life into our home. We always say we have 2 sons; one just has a different address! He has the ultimate gift we want to give all of our children...Heaven!

In closing, I would like to tell you about the anniversary of Matthew's funeral. We were on our way to the cemetery thinking of our year and the ending of it, when we turned down the road... a rainbow... yes, there it was, put there just for us. God's Promise!!! We smiled and cried as we knew that it was time for our rainbow, and God wanted to remind us on that special day of His promise! We had not seen a rainbow in so long, but at the moment when we needed it most, it was there. Beautiful, isn't it?

Have a BLESSED day! For you made a difference in our lives! Sincerely, Lori Weatherly

Happy Birthday to Me...

My birthday, the one that is centered around the 4th of July parties, celebrations and hoopla. Well, actually it hasn't always been a day of celebration for me and my family. On my 15th birthday, my brother's baby boy passed away.

The entire month of June, I had been counting down the days to when I "expected" to get my driving permit! I would be 15 and ready to legally sit behind the wheel of a car! I had "expected" to get up and fix my hair just perfect for the picture on my driving permit. But instead of standing in line at the driver's license bureau, I was standing in the hospital watching my brother hold his beautiful baby boy singing happy birthday to a baby who would never hear his daddy sing, but they were words I would never forget.

A day that I had expected to be a day of celebration turned into a day of sadness and heartache that would be followed by many more days of sadness and heartache. July 3rd used to be a day to celebrate my birthday but it would be many years before I could accept a Happy Birthday wish from anyone. Although I was tough in front of everyone, I was completely shocked by the death of my nephew, and hid it under all of the guilt I was experiencing of wanting the "happy" birthday I had expected.

As time went on, birthdays came and went... but none were ever the same. The day before my 31st birthday, is when my own son passed away. Double whammy for me and my family. When my birthday came in 2006 I dared anyone to wish me a happy birthday. I didn't want cake or presents, I just wanted it to be over. Completely over. The sounds of fireworks and laughter were just too much for me to bear. How could I possibly celebrate my birthday? The sting of death surrounding my birthday was just too painful.

What I experienced in the days leading up to Matthew's 1st birthday was horrific. The images, the screams, the cries, the pain and confusion replayed in my head repeatedly. When I closed my eyes, I saw blood; when I was in silence, I heard screams. A living nightmare, a hell I seemed to be trapped in. I couldn't even look at people who were wishing me happy birthday.

There are really no words to describe the daunting feeling of all of the "first's"... first Christmas, first Easter... first birthday. I literally felt my throat closing in and my chest tightening as Matthew's birthday approached. I still feel that way. June is a really hard month on me physically and emotionally. It takes every ounce of courage I have to face each day. It doesn't get easier but I did get better at using God's Word to rely on. I have gotten better at trusting in His promise.

As for Matthew's birthday, I decorate the cemetery, and we send our balloons up... but the longing in my heart to have him blow out his candles, even just once will never go away. It is a day of sadness for me mixed with extreme gratefulness to God for giving me the opportunity to be his mama and to have such love for him. I miss him so much.

I am still anti-happy birthday for myself. Too much pain. What I have chosen to celebrate on July 3 is life. I celebrate my life and where God has brought me and my family on this journey.

R.I.P.

When I would think of my children's future, I would think of milestones like Ronnie giving the first car speech, the first date speech, graduation speech and eventually a wedding speech, but never did I 'expect' to have to listen to my child's eulogy and pick out a monument that would mark the place where my baby boy would be laid to rest.

There is no longer walk than to walk the path a mother has to take to bury her child. And no path more frequently visited,

whether on foot or in her heart or mind, the path always lies deep within her soul.

Two years after we laid our son's body to rest in a cemetery just a few miles from our home, I was remembering some precious moments when I had an unexpected revelation.

I kept thinking about the crosses, tombstones and flower arrangements I had seen in the cemetery with R.I.P. (Rest In Peace) written on them. Those words have bothered me since Matthew's passing and I never understood why until tonight. In my grief I have learned a lot of life lessons, lessons that will last a lifetime and this was a major one!

I just kept thinking of R.I.P. and in my heart I cannot imagine Matthew resting in peace in heaven. I imagine him full of peace but I also imagine him giving the angels a run for their money... not resting. No rest for the angels either watching over him. I just got sad and became emotional over this, and it began to bother me for some reason. I had no rest in dealing with this until I heard a small gentle voice, "YOU rest in PEACE mommy." I began to sob as I realized that instruction was for me, not Matthew.

Many nights, too many to count, I have not slept, nor rested, much less in "peace," yet as I realized the tenderness of this moment, I was calmed by the crosses and the tombstones that were replaying in my mind though they had once brought disturbance to my soul. For these etched words are not for those who have left us, rather they are for those still here. As you read this, you may not agree with me, nor am I asking you to. I am just sharing what I have come to believe.

Today, when I walk to the cemetery, I will see those words Rest In Peace around me and smile knowing that my heart understands now, my heart has come full circle with those feelings and tonight when I lay down my head, I will rest in peace knowing that is exactly what Matthew wants me to do.

Psalm 4:8 says, "In peace I will both lie down and sleep, for You, Lord, alone make me dwell in safety and confident trust." (AMP)

Making peace with the place... the most special place on this earth to me is where my baby was laid to rest, just a few feet away from where my brother's baby Christopher was buried sixteen years earlier. Death and horror used to grip my soul when I would go there and now, serenity and peace envelop me. In this beautiful place of serenity are the words etched on Matthew's tombstone from 1 Samuel 1:27-28.

I prayed for this child and the Lord has granted me what I have asked of him, so now I give him back to the Lord. (NIV)

Isaiah 26:3 says, "You will guard him and keep him in perfect and constant peace whose mind [both its inclination and its character] is stayed on You, because he commits himself to You, leans on You, and hopes confidently in You. So trust in the Lord (commit yourself to Him, lean on Him, hope confidently in Him) forever; for the Lord God is an everlasting Rock [the Rock of Ages]" (AMP).

Tomorrow's almost here...

Tomorrow's almost here and already I feel
My chest tightening, it doesn't seem real.

Tomorrow's almost here and breathless I am
My heart is aching and increasingly sad.

For tomorrow there will be no ribbons or bows
No presents, no toys, no bubbles to blow.

Those things they've been traded for tears in our eyes
For in our hello, we had to tell you goodbye.

Tomorrow we will find many memories of you
As we wonder what life would bring you at two.

Tomorrow I'll close my eyes longing to hear
Your little feet in the hallway drawing near.

Tomorrow I'll remember how you felt on that day
And how when I kissed you goodbye, my heart flew away.

*Tomorrow I'll love you even more precious one
You are my sweet boy, my baby, my beloved son.*

*Tomorrow's almost here and I'll be sending balloons
Straight up to the heavens especially for you.*

*Each one will be full of hugs and kisses
Sending all of our love and birthday wishes.*

*Tomorrow's almost here and I'll be holding on tight
To make it through from morning til' night.*

*Tomorrow's almost here and it scares me so
To see the day come and yet to see it go.*

*When tomorrow's come and gone and is my yesterday
Then why will I feel the same way today?*

*Because you are my tomorrow and you are my yesterday
You are my right now, my forever, my today and always.*

*To my precious Matthew... I love and miss you eternally!
Happy 2nd Birthday!*

All my love, Mommy

Dealing with the Unexpected

In Matthew 11:28, Jesus says, "Come to Me, all you who labor and are heavy-laden and over-burdened and I will cause you to rest. [I will ease and relieve and refresh your souls.]" (AMP).

Facets of Life

Have you ever felt as though you were carrying a heavy load? _____

Have you ever felt over-burdened? _____
What has prevented you from sleeping at night? _____

What does Jesus tell us to do in Matthew 11:28 to receive rest? ____
_____

Psalm 4:8 says, "In peace I will both lie down and sleep, for You, Lord, alone make me dwell in safety and confident trust" (AMP).

Isaiah 26:3 says, "You will guard him and keep him in perfect and constant peace whose mind [both its inclination and its character] is stayed on You, because he commits himself to You, leans on You, and hopes confidently in You. So trust in the Lord (commit yourself to Him, lean on Him, hope confidently in Him) forever; for the Lord God is an everlasting Rock [the Rock of Ages]" (AMP).

The secret to being able to lie down and sleep is revealed in these two verses. Write out the secret to peaceful, restful sleep you have learned. _____

Thank your Heavenly Father for His perfect peace and rest.

Chapter Five

When God's Will became Our Will...

We planned on trying to adopt about a year after Matthew's passing. We really believed that there was a baby out there that needed us. We began the paperwork but to say we were scared was an understatement. The risks of adoption were enormous. All of the stories I read online terrified me and on top of the risks, I didn't want to wait two to four years. Now that we had decided to do this, I wanted a baby now!

My reaction to possibly being "let down" by an agency or birth-parents was this... I had already lost my son, what could hurt me worse than that? In my mind, I had nothing to lose. There was no greater hurt I could experience, so we put ourselves out there and jumped in.

My thoughts though were that we should adopt a baby girl. I never wanted to hold another baby and compare him to Matthew. I was afraid that I would always do that, so we told our social worker, ONLY a girl. Absolutely NO BOY.

An Unexpected Change in Plans

So on Saturday, September 9, 2006, when Danita, our social worker called me at 5 pm and said, "I know you told me not to call you unless I had a girl, but God just kept telling me to call you. Would you and Ronnie consider a boy?" my heart sank... Ronnie was outside so I told her I would have to call her back. I was in shock. I had thought I wouldn't even have to consider such a choice and to say I was confused was an understatement. I went to the door and called to Ronnie saying we needed to talk. We sat on the bed as I told him about the phone call and what Danita had said about the baby boy. We were freaked out, totally freaked out but took a minute to pray before we decided to call her back.

Out of my mouth came the words I had never expected to be able to say, "I want him!" In a daze, both of us sat there for a few minutes looking at each other at this newest unexpected change in plans. We both felt as though we were about to throw up and pass out all at the same time but there was also a sort of calm assurance that we were doing what God had asked us to do. Now what?

We decided not to say anything to our families until we knew more and had had some time to settle our own churning emotions. I did call my two sisters and asked them to pray that God's will be done in this as things were definitely not going as we had expected, again. All through the night, Danita kept in close contact with us as she talked with the birthmother. We didn't sleep! What would prove to be a night and day of maybe and maybe not from the birthmother kept us on a rollercoaster as we battled our own up and down emotions.

We got a call to meet at 4 pm on Sunday afternoon. We decided to call our sisters and brothers, fill them in, but stressed that we MAY be getting a baby. We asked them to arrange a party at our house just in case we did, ordering 10 pizzas and get our parents there without telling them a word. It was Grandparent's Day! We figured if we got a baby it would be the most incredible gift to give to them, not to mention what an incredible surprise it would be! None of us had expected anything to happen this quickly!

So on the way to our 4 pm meeting, <u>maybe to get a baby or maybe not</u>, we went to Wal-Mart to purchase a car seat, a baby blanket, a pack of diapers, wipes and a baby bottle. Were we really to be new parents again? These few items were all we had, but they were accompanied by a great faith that if it were God's will, we were going to have this baby boy! We ran into Ronnie's sister, Rita, in the baby department of Wal-mart getting a baby gift to bring to our house. It was kind of funny as we nervously exchanged smiles with her and a little nervous laugh. We felt like we were crazy people walking around in the baby department, looking at each other and wondering what would unfold in the next hour.

Our hearts were on the line! Our prayers were a constant stream to our God who had gotten us this far. We knew God was granting us the ability to trust Him completely, to have faith and hope in His promise without abandon. Again an unexplainable, unexpected peace settled over us.

God's Will

As we casually sat in the car with our little bag of baby items, we waited for the phone call. We tried not to get our hopes up as we discussed boy's names. We had only talked about girl's names. We kept saying if it is "God's will, then we will get him, if not then it's okay." We said that so many times within a twenty-four hour period, that we finally agreed if it was God's WILL, then it would be OUR WILL, our little William. We knew we wanted a family name for his middle name just as we had given to Nathan and Matthew, so we agreed upon William Gray Weatherly. It was perfect... IF it was God's will...

At 4 pm on Sunday, our cell phone rang as we sat in an abandoned parking lot just about a hundred feet from where the baby was, and the most beautiful words came out of Danita's mouth, "Are you ready to come and pick up your son?" WOW! We had a son! It had been twenty-three hours since Danita's first call and now, we had a son! It would be the 2nd time within a twenty-four hour period that the unexpected would change our lives forever!

Tears burst from our eyes as we rushed the few blocks to where we were to meet Danita. At three-days-old, I was handed our new baby boy. He was perfect! I could not control the tears that were flowing and the emotions were just as they were in the delivery room when I was handed our first born son, Nathan. It was all of that and more. God had just shown up and restored the joy that I thought was gone forever when Matthew left us. In that single moment, as we met our new little son, God gave Ronnie and me the greatest love imaginable for this precious tiny little boy. It was amazing! HIS amazing grace had just blessed us with HIS WILL.

Tears flowed freely among all of us in the room. The first thing I did when Danita handed William to me was gently placed his cheek upon my cheek. "He is so warm," I whispered, remembering the last tender moment I had with Matthew and the coldness against my face as I held him cheek to cheek. God is so good and faithful! I knew at that moment that I would not have to worry about comparing this child to Matthew. God had given us such great love for William that I knew we would always see him as our precious gift from our loving Father.

We left the office and had about an hour drive home. It was our alone time to get to know this precious little gift from God. We called all of our sisters and brothers and were filled with great anticipation as we thought of introducing "our son" to everyone! Nathan was at his Nay Nay's, so that would be our first stop. He would be the first to meet this newest member of our family. I still remember the way I felt when Nathan held his tiny brother, his brother that had breath, life and was here with us to love. It was the most special gift ever.

As we approached our home that we knew was filled with family members, close friends and of course, Danita the heavenly angel God sent His blessing through, we waited for one more call. Our parents had not yet arrived nor did they know why they were coming. Once all of our parents arrived, we got the signal to go home… and that we did. Our home was filled with cameras, family and joyous anticipation! Ronnie and I let Nathan hold the car seat as we slowly opened the door. All eyes were upon the baby and Nathan as Nathan proudly made his announcement, "HAPPY GRANDPARENTS DAY! WELCOME WILLIAM GRAY WEATHERLY TO OUR HOME!"

I cannot write words that even come close to adequately describing the surprise, the joy and the emotion we all felt that day. Our parents, family and friends crying tears of joy, rejoicing together with us as we welcomed our new little son. I will never forget as we all stood together in our foyer and my dad prayed over our family and this new little life God had just given to us. We were all in tears and would continue to be for many weeks to come. There has never been a greater moment in our home; I am not sure there ever will be or that there ever should be.

William, God's Will for Our Lives

Over the next twenty-four hours our home turned into one enormous baby shower. Friends, family and people we didn't even know were bringing gifts. Everything we needed; diapers, formula, clothes all began to appear. It was amazing! The generosity and love shown to us was a blessing and we will never forget it, never. God surrounded our family with so many people that loved us and rejoiced with us over the gift of life in our home.

The night we brought Will home, after everyone left, I took the blue teddy bear and as tears rolled down my face, I kissed it and hugged it, and then I placed it into a curio cabinet with all of Matthew's belongings. It was bittersweet, but I knew God was allowing me to let go of it and take care of this precious baby He had just given to us.

William, our son. God's will for our lives. It was only September but I was already looking forward to four stockings hanging on the mantle. God is so good! When we are faithful to Him and believe in His promise and His restoration and allow Him to do things in His time, He makes it all beautiful…all of it.

Don't get overwhelmed if you are facing an obstacle today. If you are waiting for God's will and it seems too hard, too long and too impossible… don't underestimate what God can do within a twenty-four hour period. Look what He did for us!

Nathan's Thoughts:

Being a big brother is one of the hardest but most enjoyable things I do.

We would pray every night to adopt a baby to love. I wanted someone here so that I would not feel lonely around the house sometimes. I felt a little bit nervous but I felt glad that my parents were going to adopt a baby when they could. I could hardly stand waiting on the day when we would adopt a baby.

When my parents were explaining adoption to me, they said that God had a baby for us somewhere and that this baby was growing in our hearts and not in my mama's belly.

I felt very special when I heard that we were going to adopt Will. I was so excited about having a brother on earth and one in heaven. Just as God saved Matthew and gave him a better life, He saved Will, because Will could have had a much different life with another family or in an orphanage. I thank God for the many blessings that He has given our family, including Will.

Will was so small he could fit in my Ole Miss football helmet. We took our first picture together dressed in Ole Miss clothes and he was in the helmet. I was so happy. He is one of the best things to ever happen to me and that is true. Being a big brother is one of the hardest but most enjoyable things I do.

God promised me a little brother and God always keeps His promises. Now Will is irritating at four-years-old, but enjoyable. No one can count how many good times we have had together. I love him very much. Thank you Jesus for blessing our family with Will.

Ronnie's Thoughts:

I am so grateful that God gave us what we needed, not what we thought we wanted!

It was a beautiful sunny September day; a good day to catch up on a few neglected things around the house. I was outside working on my tractor, one of the more enjoyable things on my "to do" list, when Lori received the call from our Social Worker.

The last few weeks had been composed of filling out forms, meeting with adoption attorneys and completing a home study. After a year, we prayed and felt impressed God wanted us to adopt. Carolina Rose was the name we had already picked out. Lori's mother was from South Carolina and my mother's name was Rose, thus Carolina Rose. The stone we picked out a few months earlier for our fireplace was even labeled Carolina Rose. I know, kind of cool. We were adamant about adopting a girl so we instructed our agency not to notify us for any boys.

In retrospect, it was fear that lead to that decision. Fear that we were trying to replace Matthew. That is the one thing we would not want to happen. Fearful others would say that God replaced Matthew with another boy.

So there I was working on my tractor when Lori called out to me that Danita had called and we needed to talk. Now mind you, we had just completed our home study the week before and had been advised it could be at least nine to eighteen months before adoption was possible.

Lori, not one to beat around the bush, simply said Danita had called and is looking for a home for a new baby boy. My first reaction was one of aggravation. We told her no boys. How could she call and do that to my wife? I tried to hide any sense of aggravation from Lori and simply told her let's spend some time in quiet and pray about it. Any time the subject of adopting a boy had brought up in the past; Lori would always cry and say, "No, she could not have another boy unless it was Matthew."

After a few minutes of quiet prayer, Lori came to me and said she really believed God wanted us to have this little baby boy. I stood there confused, not really knowing what to say. Lori had been so certain about a girl. Carolina Rose would be her name; named for our mothers and remember the stone.

So it was in this context that when we called back, I asked Danita, "Is there any reason we should not adopt this little boy?"

Now in my mind's eye, Danita was supposed to say, "Well, you did ask for a girl" or "I am sorry, I dialed the wrong number" or "there was a mix-up." But what she did say through her joyful tears was, "No, there is no reason for you guys not to adopt."

It was at that moment I realized what had just happened and tears overwhelmed me. God had blessed us with Will. He knew the desire of our hearts even when we didn't recognize them. Will has been a miracle for us in so many ways. My expectations were different than what God had in store for us. I am so grateful that God didn't give us what we wanted, but instead gave us what we needed.

There are times in our lives when our expectations are not met. This can lead to disappointment or, in our case, nearly missing God's will altogether. In Luke Chapter 24 on the road to Emmaus, two others were faced with how to handle unmet expectations. They were so blinded by their disappointment that they failed to see Jesus was right there with them. They were looking for Jesus to come and redeem Israel. Instead Jesus had died in order to be resurrected and save all of humanity. They looked for a ruler but were met with a savior. Their unmet expectations led to doubt and in that setting Jesus reminded them of His plans and then revealed Himself to them.

How many times have we allowed our disappointment to affect what God has in store for us? If it was not for Lori's willingness to look beyond her expectations and look for God's expectations, we would have missed out on our Will, which was God's will. I pray in earnest that my expectations are His expectations, that His will is my will.

Danita's Thoughts:

I am trying to type through the tears in my eyes because I can remember this like it happened today. I have practiced social work for numerous years and until Will I had never faced a situation like this. I had a family paired with his birthmother up until his birth. They changed their mind on the 2nd day. Will was a full term, healthy child with no drug exposure. It is unheard of since for every one child born I have 10 couples waiting. I called 3 other couples but the entire time I heard the Lord say Lori, but I continued to ignore His word. I even held my hand over the receiver and said out loud; Lord you know they only want a daughter. So I said to the Lord, I will show you. Still not willing to obey, I called Lori's sister Lynette, a friend of mine. I knew she would say no don't call Lori and I could have the last word. She hesitated for a period but said call her.

When I called Lori I started with an apology, "I know you said a girl but the Lord continues to put your name on my heart so I can't ignore Him any longer. Now, I will allow you to decide."

My thought was I will let you show Him that I was right. I remember being so fearful that this would not happen and I would be the person responsible for more pain in Ronnie and Lori's lives. I continued to pray for them and Will's amazing birthmother. I prayed for peace for all of them. I asked God to give strength and peace to the Lori, Ronnie and the birthmother. Out of the blue, Lori called and answered one of my prayers.

She said, "I don't want you to worry if this doesn't work out. It has given me joy for a day and I realize how much I do want to adopt. An amazing woman (his birthmother) loved a little boy enough to give him a wonderful life that she was unable to provide."

There is no way that Will's life could have been any better. He is definitely with the right family. I was humbled to realize God has a plan for our lives if we just obey Him.

Our Lives have been Forever Changed

When Will was six weeks old, we dedicated him and had a huge celebration! On the invitations were the words:

"God's Will" became our "Will"
Our lives have been forever changed twice within 24 hours,
this time leaving smiles instead of sadness and joy instead of sorrow.
"Whoever accepts a child in my name accepts me." Matthew 18:5

Dealing with the Unexpected

Ronnie asked a very important question at the end of this chapter, one we each need to carefully reflect on.

How many times have we allowed our disappointment to affect what God has in store for us?_____

In Luke Chapter 24:19-24, read how two of Jesus' disciple explained their unmet expectations to the stranger they did not recognize as the Lord Himself.

> *And He said to them, "What things?" And they said to Him, "The things about Jesus the Nazarene, who was a prophet mighty in deed and word in the sight of God and all the people, and how the chief priests and our rulers delivered Him to the sentence of death, and crucified Him. But we were hoping that it was He who was going to redeem Israel. Indeed, besides all this, it is the third day since these things happened. But also some women among us amazed us. When they were at the tomb early in the morning, and did not find His body, they came, saying that they had also seen a vision of angels who said that He was alive. Some of those who were with us went to the tomb and found it just exactly as the women also had said; but Him they did not see."* (NAS)

What had they expected Jesus to do? _____

_____

How did they respond when He didn't do what they expected Him to? _____

_____

Even when Jesus explained that He did exactly what God's plan had called for, they still could not see beyond their disappointment and realize they were speaking with the Lord, Himself!

And He said to them, "O foolish men and slow of heart to believe in all that the prophets have spoken! Was it not necessary for the Christ to suffer these things and to enter into His glory?" Then beginning with Moses and with all the prophets, He explained to them the things concerning Himself in all the Scriptures. (Luke 24:25-27 NAS)

It was not until they sat quietly at the table with Jesus that they were finally able to see Him. Then they realized something we all need to remember about our loving Heavenly Father. Underline the secret they reveal to us about knowing God's will for our lives.

And they said to one another, "Were not our hearts greatly moved and burning within us while He was talking with us on the road and as He opened and explained to us [the sense of] the Scriptures?" (Luke 24:32AMP)

We need to pray as Jesus Christ Himself did the night before His trial and crucifixion.

And going a little farther, He threw Himself upon the ground on His face and prayed saying, My Father, if it is possible, let this cup pass away from Me; nevertheless, not what I will [not what I desire], but as You will and desire. (Matthew 26:39 AMP)

What Jesus is teaching us here is that it is alright to tell God we are hurting, disappointed and confused but then we also must tell God that we want what He wants for our lives even is it is not what we expect. No matter what the circumstances are in your life, take the time to sit with Jesus, open your heart up to Him, tell Him how you feel but then declare you want God's will for your life. It will change your life forever!

Chapter Six

Barna Belles - The Great Encouragers

In life before our tragedy, I had been very active in church, in women's ministry and devoted to making a difference in the lives of others. Now that I was pretty much homebound due to my injuries, I felt handicapped and wondered how God could ever use me. Even as the thought crossed my mind, I wondered if I even still had a passion for hurting ladies anymore. My heart, though in constant pain, had grown so cold and seemingly impervious to the suffering of others. I was afraid that since I was unable to attend church on a regular basis that my time in ministry was over. I was also afraid that I had been hurt so bad that a compassion for others would never come back. I was still so angry that others had their babies and I had lost mine that reaching out to others seemed nearly impossible. I was still plagued by so many crazy thoughts and conflicting emotions that I couldn't even help myself much less minister to someone else.

As God began to stir my heart to start a home ministry, I felt fear rise up inside of me. I feared letting people into my life again. I feared letting them see me in a "weak" way. When I looked at what I used to be, I was afraid they would only pity me or worse yet, I would feel that overwhelming jealousy that they had what I could never have again. Before I was so strong, always going full throttle but now I was different. I didn't like the new me, so how could they? I knew that in order to minister to others I would have to open my life up to them.

I also knew I was still full of anger and embarrassed by my physical condition. What would they think if they saw what was really going on inside of me? I couldn't seem to help myself, how could God think I could help others? Why would God want others to see the hurt in my eyes? Why would He want me to share such painful experiences with others? I had lost so much; my life, my dignity, and my hope. How could someone as lost as me help anyone else?

I could not even begin to understand why God wanted me to do this, but I confided in two of my friends, Shawn and Tina, what God had been laying on my heart. I didn't know why or how I was going to do this but I knew God wanted me to proceed. I was amazed when they not only encouraged me to go forward with what God was telling me, but that they would work with me to reach out to other women in the area. So with fear in my every step, we planned to have our first meeting here in my home in October of 2006. We wanted to allow God to open our hearts to become what would be known as the Barna Belles. The name was derived from Barnabus, the great encourager of Acts. Our vision for this ministry was just that, we were to be encouragers.

God is Amazing!

Little did I know that God was going to give us little Will in September, just four weeks before the date of our first Barna Belles meeting. The night that the ladies walked into my house, they came with gifts... gifts for our son! These were the same ladies that had brought gifts to my baby shower for Matthew. But now they were walking in my home bearing gifts for Will! God is amazing! I stood there holding William in front of the ladies that I had not seen since losing Matthew and I sobbed as I gave my testimony. My heart opened, I felt free to love each one of them, and found that, yes, God could use me! For the first time, God's purpose and plan was clear to me for my new life and a new ministry. I was full of fear as I spoke of the tragedy, yet I stood firm in God and in faith that He was there with me.

For about two years, the Barna Belles met monthly, shared online devotionals, prayer requests, raised money for needy families and did outreaches to those hurting or in need. We reached people all over the world through our prayer and card ministry. It was awesome and each lady was so very special to me. It was therapy at home for me as I prayed for the lives of so many others daily. I grew stronger in my faith and that was just what the Great Physician ordered. As He had so lovingly done in our lives before, God gave us what we needed, not what we thought we wanted.

I often think of the words I read in a Max Lucado book in regards to the two maestros who sat listening to a talented young girl sing. They looked at each other and said she would sing much better after her heart had been broken.[7] I understand now what they were saying because the brokenness in my heart has driven me to desperate measures and to places I never would have dreamed I would go; some good, some bad. But these places have ultimately left me totally dependent upon God, and there is no better place to go with a broken heart. Only God can refine and perfect what was once a mess, so it can be used for His glory.

This letter was written to the Barna Belles on June 4, 2007, less than a month away from Matthew's 2nd birthday.

I am not quite sure where to begin today, as much is on my heart. Last week when I was in time out (taking a break), God shared several things that I have to rely on to get me through the next month. Although I will not be sharing it all with you, I will share the pieces that perhaps may touch you as well.

The grief my heart has been feeling lately over the loss of Matthew has taken me back yet again to the place that fear and uncertainty in life can lead. As July 2nd is approaching, I feel my chest tightening and I want to run away. I want to run away from the hurt, the memories, the sickness, the heartache, the tears... but I cannot; for they are part of my life. They are the bridge between my then and now... If I run away from them, I run away from the healing that God is giving to me. I run away from the opportunity of reaching someone

---

[7] taken from Max Lucado, A Gentle Thunder, Word Publishing, Dallas, Texas, copyright 1995

that is sick or that is grieving over the loss of a child and needs to know Jesus cares for them and will hold them when they need to be held. So instead of running away, I ran to Jesus. For when one is unreachable to others, it is then Jesus holds them the closest. Today, He is doing that for me.

I knew last week I needed to crawl into the lap of Jesus and just talk to Him, share my fears and cry a while on His shoulder, and I did just that. And in return, He held me, He comforted me and wiped my tears. He listened to me and He heard my request. I was sure to go to Him with thanksgiving in my heart as instructed in Philippians 4:6, 'Do not be anxious about anything, but in everything, by prayer and petition, with thanksgiving, present your requests to God.'

I recognized my weakness; I knew I had to return to the only place that could give me strength to go on. Isaiah 40:29-31 encouraged me as well. 'He gives strength to the weary and increases the power of the weak. Even youths grow tired and weary and young men stumble and fall; but those who hope in the Lord will renew their strength. They will soar on wings like eagles; they will run and not grow weary, they will walk and not be faint.'

I know the next month will be hard for me and I know I cannot try to walk through this, so I have asked God to carry me... and as much as my heart has hurt and been broken and my mind may replay the events of that tragic night, and I don't understand any of it, this verse was given to me for this time in my life and brings much comfort to me. I have to have peace, especially since I do not understand the past two years. I have to know that my hurting heart is protected, and that my mind, where so many nightmares manifest is guarded. I have that promise in the verse below.

Philippians 4:7, 'And the peace of God which transcends all understanding will guard your hearts and minds in Christ Jesus.'

Love to all, Lori

My dear friend Shawn's thoughts on the Barna Belles:

God had been speaking to Lori and me both about starting a women's ministry although neither of us knew it until one day Lori mentioned what God was laying on her heart to do. Thus the "Barna-Belles" ministry was born. The year leading up to the start of the Barna-Belles was a tumultuous one for many families along the Mississippi Gulf Coast because of Hurricane Katrina. Lori and I both had been part of a strong women's ministry prior to that devastating storm. After the storm ravaged the area, many of the women we fellowshipped with were scattered. Many of the churches were operating as best they could after so many people were scattered or even homeless. As a result the women's ministries were suffering as well.

My family and I evacuated for the approaching hurricane with three days worth of clothes on our backs, only to return home to a house that had 13 feet of water. We were not only faced with rebuilding our home by both my husband and I were also laid off from our jobs as a result of the storm. We had lost our home and now our means of providing for our family as well. I tell you, in spite of the trouble we faced, as I thought of all my best friend had lost, I never felt sorry for us or our family. What Lori was going through with the loss of her son and the physical pain she was faced with every day was greater than I could even imagine.

Out of the ashes of Lori's loss and the extreme devastation of our beloved home towns, a ministry of encouragement was born. The Barna-Belles was a healing process for many that participated. I had always been told that the best way to get your mind off of your own problems was to help others. That is exactly what we did and we did indeed receive healing for our own souls.

Jeremiah 29:11 became my battle cry! God gave me that verse on many occasions as I faced life's trials. "'I know the plans I have for you,' declares the Lord, 'plans to prosper you and not to harm you, plans to give you hope and a future.'"[8]

In researching this verse I learned that "prosper" actually means peace. In God's eyes to prosper means to have peace. How cool is

---

[8] NIV

that! I so needed peace in my life and so did so many other women all around us. In my kitchen I have a picture hanging on the wall that is titled, "Be Encouraged" and below it is written this verse from Jeremiah 29:11. I pray every day as I look at that picture that we would be able to do just that as we carry out God's ministry; reaching across denominations to encourage and touch women's lives for God's Glory.

The Barna-Belle ministry is never far from my heart or memory. Many women were blessed by God's touching hand because other women were willing to be used for His glory, despite their own situations at home. It is simply amazing how God works!

As Shawn said above, the Barna Belle ministry will never be far from my heart or my memory either. It was a very special time for me, and I am so thankful to her and Tina for taking such care of the ministry when it was time for me to step away to have my surgeries.

My Legacy of Faith

As Ronnie shared in an earlier chapter, God had seen to it I had a foundation of faith on which to build long before we faced the unexpected events of the summer of 2005. I want to share with you the legacy of faith God had given me even as a child knowing I would need this strong foundation in order to fulfill His purpose and plan for the new life and new ministry I would be called to move into. Even though I wavered and dealt with a myriad of conflicting emotions, I stood firm in God and in the faith that I was grounded in even as a child.

Growing up as a preacher's daughter, I was able to see God's grace on a daily basis. My parents were dependent upon God's grace and their faith to provide for a family of five on a preacher's salary. My father had a massive stroke when I was only 11 years old. Being the baby of our family, I didn't understand why God allowed this to happen to him or my family. I saw my super-hero preacher daddy, that did all he could do to serve God, turn into a man who had to relearn his alphabet and even our names all over again. It was a terrible time for our family and a lot of asking God WHY?

HOW could this happen? If my dad served God with all of his heart and God allowed him to have a stroke, then why do I want to serve Him? Why put so much faith in someone who could allow such disappointment and heartache? I was crushed and my faith was sorely tested. The stroke paralyzed my dad's whole right side and it took him years in therapy to learn to function again. He is still paralyzed, but at 72 years old he still inspires me to press on and do what I have to do with what I have and leave the rest to God. He always said, "If God fails me this time, it will be the first time."

That would have to be one of my most quoted statements over the last five years. My dad could have blamed God, and walked away from Him, but he CHOSE not to. My mother never lost faith that, in all things God works for the good of those who love him, who have been called, according to his purpose.[9] Despite tragedy, my parents never gave up on faith but instead their faith grew and prospered and when grace was all they had to hold on to, it was enough. That's why they call it "Amazing Grace…" The testimony that God has given them over the years has encouraged and helped the lives of so many. _There is nothing that you are expecting today or NOT expecting that God is not preparing you for._

As I became a wife and a mother, I began to look back and see the many blessings God gave us when tragedy stuck our family as I was growing up. Sometimes it takes many years to see the blessings though we may never understand all the "whys." But I can tell you that in the past twenty-six years, many lives have been changed because of my dad and mom's faith; a constant faith that was reflected in their lives and spilled over into our home and into the lives of so many others. They taught me that when we live by faith, God's grace is sufficient for all our needs.[10] Faith and grace…great teachers for how we are to live in the world today.

What I am now teaching my boys and hoping that they see in us, is what was modeled in my childhood home. It is not just that we need faith and grace to live our lives, but without faith it is impos-

---

[9] See Romans 8:28

[10] See 2 Corinthians 12:9

sible to please God.[11] It is critical for our faith that we accept God's grace in our lives and extend it to others as well. Then, and only then, can we have the faith that gives us the hope to live, no matter what the trial is that we are walking in.

The prayer I always prayed over my children when I was pregnant was a simple; "Dear Lord, please keep my baby safe, healthy and happy and with us always." God answered that prayer, even on the day Matthew was born, He held him and took him safely home, where he is safe, healthy and happy and where we will be with him always in eternity. I still pray those words over my boys every night and they bring great comfort to me, and my boys. There is something about hearing your mama pray over you... my mother was an incredible example of a praying mama, and she still is!

---

[11] See Hebrews 11:6

Strength for Dealing with the Unexpected

Our experience has been life changing across the board. God has given us such wonderful treasures and blessings along the broken road and the sweet memories and moments that bring a smile to our faces or tears to our eyes. We have learned to cherish them all. Most everything in our lives has changed, but GOD HAS NOT. He has never left us or forsaken us. On a daily basis, God teaches me through the trials and tragedies in our lives that building upon faith, learning from mistakes and loving through it all is a definite must!

There were a lot of days I felt like Job in the Bible, and I still do sometimes. In Job 16:5-6 it says, "But my mouth would encourage you, comfort from my lips would bring you relief. Yet if I speak, my pain is not relieved and if I refrain, it does not go away." But I also learned from studying the life of Job that God has a restoration plan for those who choose to love Him through whatever trials we face in life. God's restoration plan for Job far exceeded my *expectations*. What God has restored to us may not have been what I *expected* or how I *expected* it, but God is so good. Regardless of what my circumstances look like to me, He has given us this amazing promise in Jeremiah 29:11-14.

> *"For I know the plans I have for you," declares the LORD, "plans to prosper you and not to harm you, plans to give you hope and a future. Then you will call upon me and come and pray to me, and I will listen to you. You will seek me and find me when you seek me with all your heart. I will be found by you," declares the LORD, "and will bring you back from captivity. I will gather you from all the nations and places where I have banished you," declares the LORD, "and will bring you back to the place from which I carried you into exile."* (NIV)

Restoration is a painful procedure, but if you are in a position of unexpected heartache, you must trust God to restore what has ripped you open inside. You must be willing, at all costs, to find a way to let go and let God restore your brokenness and begin to heal your heartache. Isaiah 41:9-14 has given me great comfort as I have walked through this restoration process.

> *I took you from the ends of the earth, from its farthest corners I called you. I said, 'You are my servant'; I have chosen you and have not rejected you. So do not fear, for I am with you; do not be dismayed, for I am your God. I will strengthen you and help you; I will uphold you with my righteous right hand... For I am the LORD, your God, who takes hold of your right hand and says to you, Do not fear; I will help you. Do not be afraid, O worm Jacob, O little Israel, for I myself will help you," declares the LORD, your Redeemer, the Holy One of Israel.* (NIV)

I often turn to Psalm 23:1-3 and read this beautiful portrait of Jesus Christ, my loving shepherd. "The Lord is my Shepherd, I shall not want. He makes me lie down in green pastures, he leads me beside still waters, He restores my soul..."[12] When all is chaotic in my world, I can find peace in Him. Jesus Himself told us we would face trouble and trials in this world.[13] But God has promised us that He can and WILL restore our souls!

Matthew Taught Me to Love

I thought that because I had to let Matthew go that my love would for some reason not be able to hold on. I was wrong and in time, I began to love as I had never loved before, appreciating every moment and every breath of life. When you can no longer touch someone, it doesn't mean you can no longer love them or that your heart becomes disconnected. It is actually just the opposite. When you cannot physically feel someone's heart beat, the touch of their hand or see a tear in their eye, it just drives you to find out just how big and how powerful love is and can be once it is understood. Letting go means loving... loving more than you ever imagined.

---

[12] NIV

[13] See John 16:32

I believe love is a God-given gift to comfort us. I love Matthew just as much as I love my other boys. I never heard him cry, I never kissed his skinned knee, but I kissed him goodbye. In that kiss there was a transfer of love into another realm; one I never knew existed, but one I truly believe in and find comfort in. It is a realm I know, that without the loss of Matthew, I never would have experienced or known.

Love has become a great teacher for me.

Love is patient, love is kind. It does not envy, it does not boast, it is not proud. It is not rude, it is not self-seeking, it is not easily angered, it keeps no record of wrongs. Love does not delight in evil but rejoices with the truth. It always protects, always trusts, always hopes, always perseveres. Love never fails....
(1 Corinthians 13:4-8 NIV)

God is love and without love, there is no God. Without God, there is no hope and without hope, there can be no faith, and without faith there can be no peace. 1 Corinthians 13:13 says, "And now these three remain: faith, hope and love. But the greatest of these is love" (NIV).

Dealing with the Unexpected

Love has become a great teacher for me.

Love is patient, love is kind. It does not envy, it does not boast, it is not proud. It is not rude, it is not self-seeking, it is not easily angered, it keeps no record of wrongs. Love does not delight in evil but rejoices with the truth. It always protects, always trusts, always hopes, always perseveres. Love never fails....
(1 Corinthians 13:4-8 NIV)

This powerful scripture is actually a list of what love is and does as well as what it is not and does not do. Make two lists based on this scripture; a "to do" list and a "not to do" list. At the end of each day, check off what you did do and circle what you still need to work on.

At the beginning of this chapter, we chose a name for our women's ministry that described our mission statement. What was that name and what did it mean?

_____

What type of ministry has God called you to? _____

_____

If you do not know, then begin praying and asking God what it is He wants you to do. Don't be surprised if He uses the trials and tribulations you have walked through to minister to others. Be willing to share your testimony and God's love and mercy as it applies to what He has helped you to personally walk through in your life.

Take a few minutes to write out your own personal testimony of God's great love in your life. Always have this ready to share when God sends a hurting person across your path. You will be amazed at the healing you receive when you are willing to reach out to others.

Chapter Seven

The Fear Factor

As July, 2007 passed, and I still struggled daily with so many medical problems, I knew I needed a life that would allow me to be more active with our children. It had been 2 years now and my injuries were still substantial with complete sensory loss to the back of my legs all the way down to my feet, my bladder and bowel; still neurogenic. I had been through physical therapy, bladder therapy and focused on doing all that I could to maintain myself under the conditions I had now been living with for 2 years.

The nerve damage was very extensive and had started affecting the overall pain level. Atrophy and muscle loss was taking a toll on me. With each day the neuropathy grew more and more painful. I began to fear for my future and the quality of life I would have if this pattern continued. The hopes of the nerves regenerating were almost non-existent, so I began to seriously consider surgical options. I just knew God would heal me and I wouldn't need surgery but I was becoming more and more upset, feeling God was letting me down. I was wrong to think that, but I am human and I still had some growing to do. I had days when I would wake up and say this is the day God is going to heal me. Then I would cry myself to sleep that night because He didn't. It was a cycle that repeated often during this time as I fought the fear and tried to stand in faith. I grew anxious knowing I had to walk by faith and trust God to show me how to travel down the road I did not want to take.

As God led me to schedule the surgery, He began once again to show me He did things His way and in His timing. All I had to do was trust Him to use whatever and whomever He chose to accomplish His plan and purpose in my life. A week or so before my surgery I wrote this letter to the Barna Belles:

I have a book that was given to me when I got out of the hospital- and it is written by **Kenneth / Gloria Copeland** *entitled* **Pursuit of His Presence.** *It is a daily devotional that has dates so you can have one all year long to encourage you in life. Well, as maybe some of you do... I do this often- on a big day I always look ahead into what that date may say in this devotional book- and many, many times it is just what I need to read to remind me that God will sustain me and that this is the direction that God is leading me into.*

Well, last week when I got my surgery date confirmed.... I came home and sat in my office... grabbed my devotional book and went straight to Oct. 29th for I knew God had this planned- this date, this time... and I expectantly opened the pages to read the following- And as you all know my fear of the doctors, hospitals, and the 'unknown' happening.... much fear--- and this was great confirmation and peace that God had given to me in writing--- So I will quote it to you and I do make one change as it was written just for me! I will begin it with

DEAR LORI....

HE WILL SEE YOU THROUGH - Kenneth Copeland

Psalm 118:6- "The Lord is on my side, I will not fear."

Notice in Psalm 118:6 that David didn't say, "I'll pray and ask God to take the fear away." He didn't say, "I try not to be afraid." He said, "I WILL NOT FEAR."
Refusing to fear is first of all a matter of the will. But as that verse indicates, it is also a matter of choosing to believe that in

every situation God is on your side and by His power He will see you through.

Of course, to successfully walk by faith and not fear, we need to know exactly how to tap into that power. 2 Peter 1:3-4 tells us:

- *"His [God's] divine power hath given unto us all things that pertain unto life and godliness, through the knowledge of him that hath called us to glory and virtue:*
- *Whereby are given unto us exceeding great and precious promises: that by these ye might be partakers of the divine nature, having escaped the corruption that is in the world through lust."*

God makes everything available we could possibly need, every conceivable blessing, through the promises in His Word. If we'll believe them and activate the Law of the Spirit of Life, those promises will manifest into our lives. They will open the way for us to escape the destruction brought into the earth by the Law of Sin and Death.

Satan, however, challenges those promises with fear. He brings us contrary circumstances to convince us those promises can never come to pass. He tells us lies. He contradicts the word of God and says, "You'll never make it. You're too weak. Other people can walk by faith because they are stronger than you. You don't have the background they have. There's something wrong with you." And so on.

But no matter what, the choice is still yours. You can listen to the word of God or the lies of the devil. Which will it be?

"But Brother Copeland, I am not really listening to the devil. I believe the word of God. But I can't just forget what happened to me in the past. I failed. I didn't receive my healing. I was mistreated....."

You'd better forget those things! You'd better put them under the blood of Jesus and wash them away forever. If you don't, you'll find yourself meditating on them. And just as faith comes by hearing and hearing by the word of God, fear comes by hearing the word of the devil. Fear comes when you entertain his threats about the future and his boasts about the past.

So make the right choice... even if you have to make it every 60 seconds. Don't let the devil's lies swirl through your head for even a minute. Fill your thoughts with God's word.... remember He is on your side and will see you through.

SPEAK THE WORD- THE LORD IS ON MY SIDE- I DO NOT FEAR[14]

I have struggled with fear of surgery for over two years now and I know it is the time for me to be healed physically but also mentally of the fear I have with doctors and hospitals. And making the decision to set a date for surgery was so hard... because Satan places fear and thoughts into my head that I have to take captive and present them right back to the only person who can take away those fears... so I am doing that right now- sometimes every 60 seconds as suggested above, but nonetheless, I am doing it! I am forgetting the past and placing it under the blood of Jesus and pressing on to the prize ahead!

1 Peter 5:7- 11 says, "Cast <u>all your</u> anxiety on Him because He cares for you. Be self-controlled and alert. Your enemy the devil prowls around like a roaring lion looking for someone to devour. Resist him, standing firm in the faith, because you know that your brothers throughout the world are undergoing the same kind of sufferings. <u>And the God of all grace, who called you to His eternal glory in Christ, after you have suffered a little while, will Himself restore you and make you strong, firm and steadfast. To Him be the power forever and ever. Amen.</u>

I am expecting nothing less than a very successful surgery and a miraculous recovery and healing! Thank you for all of your prayers

---

[14] Pursuit of His Presence, Kenneth and **Gloria Copeland,** Published by Harrison House, Inc., Tulsa Oklahoma, copyright 1998

and I will chat with you soon! And I plan to be cheering for Nate at his football game on Saturday!! (I already had a talk with Jesus, He knows I cannot miss his football games!!!)

Philippians 1:6 says, He who has started a good work in you will bring it through to completion!

Love to all...Lori

Yes, to Surgery

In November of 2008, I had my first surgery for a trial inter-stem device. Nine days later, the implant was successfully implanted permanently. My doctors had been talking to me for a couple of years in regards to this surgery but I was too frightened to ever go back to the operating room. When I came out the last time, the results ended my life as I knew it. Fear and anxiety had been my best friends anytime the doctors spoke of surgery. I was afraid to trust the doctor(s) with my life.

After much prayer I realized God was using this time to show me I had to trust in HIM, and not the doctors. Once I did, I was able to say yes to the surgery. In the operating room, I laid upon the bed quoting 2 Timothy 1:7, "For God has not given me a spirit of fear, but of power and of love and of a sound mind." I said it over and over, and that was the last thought I had before I went out. It was my first thought when I woke to find out it was over! I eventually was able to build a solid relationship with the wonderful team of doctors at Ochsner. God had restored that trust in me knowing I desperately needed it in order to move forward with peace of mind. But it was a God-given peace and in His perfect timing. And, as God always does with me, He taught me a valuable lesson along the way.

The following was a closure in our 2008 Thanksgiving newsletter. It is a beautiful summary of how we felt at that time in our lives, and still how we feel today.

Throughout the past 3 years, we have learned so much. We know the importance of loving with all of your heart, we know the pain of letting go and we know the necessity of taking a risk even though you are unsure of the outcome. For in those three elements lies the true test of faith... trusting God. He sees what we cannot, and in that comes a great peace that we have also learned we cannot live without.

We are so thankful for the difference this year has made in our lives and in our home. After all of the rain, our rainbow is now before us and we gratefully embrace the beauty of it all.

Fall 2009

I was on my way to get Nate from school one day in late fall of 2009 and I heard an interview on the radio with Selah concerning their new album. They were being asked about the background of each song on the album and one song called, "I Will Carry You" instantly brought tears to my eyes. "People say that I am brave but I'm not, truth is I'm barely hanging on."[15] I felt like they knew me and what I was going through. As I sobbed, I had to drive past the school to try and compose myself before I picked Nate up. I knew at that moment I had to have that CD. Once I purchased the CD, I read the inside cover and knew once again, God knew just what I needed.

There was a picture of three little girls with their backs to the camera, sitting in front of Cinderella's castle, all with Mickey Mouse hats on. One little hat was sitting on the ground beside them. The empty hat had been embroidered with their baby sister's name who was not yet born, but not expected to live. That image, the story of her birth and passing, along with the words to that beautiful song had a powerful effect on me and where I was in my life at that time. "There were photographs I wanted to take, things I wanted to show you, sing sweet lullabies, wipe your teary eyes, who could <u>love you</u> like this?"[16]

We were in the midst of planning our own Disney trip and I knew that I would like to get my boys, all 3 of them, Mickey Mouse hats and have a memory picture like that of my own. I made that a priority at the top of my list for Disney.

---

[15] Taken from "I Will Carry You" by Selah
[16] Taken from "I Will Carry You" by Selah

Up to this point, I had not been looking forward to our trip to Disney. As a matter of fact, I had been dreading it. We spent a week at Disney when I was six months pregnant with Nathan and a week when I was pregnant with Matthew. I went back this time, not pregnant, but handicapped. I knew how much walking would be involved, as well as the amount of standing in lines that accompanied a trip to Disney World. I was afraid I wouldn't be able to walk around without chronic pain and was concerned my legs wouldn't be able to hold me up after just a few hours of walking and standing on hard cement.

I dreaded the trip, but not for just my disability. The last time I was at Disney, I had a new little life inside of me, a life that I would never get to take to Disney again. I was pregnant with Matthew though I didn't know it until we returned home from that trip. All the while we talked about going back to Disney I was screaming to myself, I can't do it... I don't want to do it! I wanted to remember Disney just as it was last time, when all was well; before the unexpected had changed our lives forever.

Pain, Tears and Memories

December 31st, 2009, we loaded our boys into the Navigator and headed for Disney World in Orlando! It was hard to tell who was more excited, my two boys or my husband! We arrived on New Year's Day and went right to the Magic Kingdom. As we walked through the gate, my heart sank as the laughter and smiles filled everyone's faces but mine. I tried, but inside I was dying, completely and quietly dying. I didn't see magic... I saw myself four years ago walking around, strong and healthy with Matthew inside of me. It was a silent hell.

I didn't share this with Ronnie. I didn't want him to see me hurting. I wanted him to just enjoy the moment with Nathan and Will. As we walked around, the tension eased and I began to loosen up. I tried so hard to forget the past and appreciate the moment. There were times I was successful, but then the physical pain would suddenly strike me and I would think about how much Matthew would have loved Disney, and about how much I wished he were with us.

Facets of Life

It was painful emotionally and physically but the medication I took helped me make it through the days as I watched my family enjoy their special time together. Two nights before we were scheduled to leave, we went back to the Magic Kingdom so that the boys could each make their own Mickey Mouse hat. We walked into the store and there were several workers around eager to help. I explained to Will and Nate that they could each make their own hat and then they each needed to pick out an ear for Matthew's hat so they could make his together. As they began to work excitedly on their designs, tears filled my eyes. My heart was beating fast as waves of grief threatened to overwhelm me.

I was about to explode with all of my emotions when a gentleman standing to the right of me caught my eye. What I didn't realize was the workers had been quietly listening and watching us. When I looked into the eyes of this man, a calm peace came over my soul. I wiped the tears that were rolling down my face and turned to look around me. Every thing seemed to be moving in slow motion. In the middle of Main Street Magic Kingdom the parade was passing by, people were laughing and clapping but I couldn't hear the laughter or the music anymore. There was only the sound of my teardrops falling to the floor...

We walked up to the checkout counter and I held three hats in my hand. As I placed them up on the counter, Nate told the man he would like to have "Moose" written on his hat. The man smiled but said they were only allowed to embroider proper names, no nick names and that he was sorry. Nate said that was alright and agreed to have "Nate" embroidered on his.

Then Nate picked up Matthew's hat and handed it to the man with the kind eyes and said, "This is for my brother Matthew, he passed away."

There went my composure. It was over... grief won. The man looked at me and kindly said he would do Matthew's hat for us at no charge. Barely able to say thank you, I put my head down and cried. The man with the kind eyes asked Ronnie if he could hug me. Ronnie said of course. When this man with the kind eyes hugged me, I knew he was an angel of mercy. God was showing me incredible mercy and using this man to minister to my broken heart in a hat store at Disney World.

God Remembers

As we left that shop on Main Street and entered the parade route, I still couldn't believe God had just used "Bob" to show me He hadn't forgotten about me. All week while we were surrounded by families laughing and playing, I had asked God if anyone remembered but me? Am I the only one who remembers Matthew was ALIVE when we were here last time? Does anyone understand the pain these memories bring? God heard my prayer and He assured me that He remembered! God remembered! God sent an angel to me to comfort me on Main Street USA in Magic Kingdom. God is so good!

The hats were sent to our room the next day and they were priceless! I took a photo of the boys with them on with Matthew's sitting next to them just like I had imagined. Well, almost; they wouldn't let me take their picture in front of Cinderella's castle, but I got the memory picture!

The day we checked out, a letter from Bob was waiting for us at the concierge's desk. I opened it and began to sob once again as I realized that he really was an angel sent by God! Our family angel that God sent to us just when we needed him. The letter was encouraging, inspiring and a treasure for all of us. In the letter, he referred to Nathan as "Moose," no proper name... it was as if he had known us forever... perhaps he had. I will never forget Bob!

The chorus from "I Will Carry You" by Selah still touches my heart!

> I will carry you,
> While your heart beats here,
> Long beyond the empty cradle,
> Through the coming years,
> I will carry you,
> All <u>my life</u>,
> I will praise the One,
> Who's chosen me,
> To carry you.

Dealing with the Unexpected

Psalm 118:6- The Lord is on my side, I will not fear...

Notice David didn't say, "I'll pray and ask God to take the fear away." He didn't say, "I try not to be afraid." He said "I WILL NOT FEAR." Do you have something you need to face today and declare, "I will not fear"? _____

2 Timothy 1:7 says, "For God has not given me a spirit of fear, but of power and of love and of a sound mind." In your own words describe the difference between living under a spirit of fear and living under the power and love of God with a sound mind.

Whatever your fear, whatever you are having trouble trusting God for, allow these scriptures to minister to your heart as they did to mine. As you read them, write down what each one does to move you closer to overcoming the fear factor in your life.

1 John 4:18 - *There is no fear in love [dread does not exist], but full-grown (complete, perfect) love turns fear out of doors and expels every trace of terror! For fear brings with it the thought of punishment, and [so] he who is afraid has not reached the full maturity of love [is not yet grown into love's complete perfection].*[17]

---

[17] AMP

Facets of Life

Luke 12:7 - *But [even] the very hairs of your head are all numbered. Do not be struck with fear or seized with alarm; you are of greater worth than many [flocks] of sparrows.*[18]

Isaiah 41:10 - *Fear not [there is nothing to fear], for I am with you; do not look around you in terror and be dismayed, for I am your God. I will strengthen and harden you to difficulties, yes, I will help you; yes, I will hold you up and retain you with My [victorious] right hand of rightness and justice. [Acts 18:10.]*[19]

Psalm 118:6 - *The Lord is on my side; I will not fear. What can man do to me? [Heb. 13:6.]*[20]

---

[18] AMP

[19] AMP

[20] *The amplified Bible, containing the amplified Old Testament and the amplified New Testament.* 1987. The Lockman Foundation: La Habra, CA

Chapter Eight

The Disappointment Factor

In March of 2009, I went in for another surgery for my bladder. Once again, quoting 2 Timothy 1:7, I went into the operating room. Another success, yet a success that did not come without risk; a risk I was aware of and willing to take. A trade off for me with this surgery was self-catheterization, not just for one day, or three weeks, but for a lifetime. It took some adjusting and depression was a constant battle during that adjustment period. Still is sometimes, but the quality of life has improved so much for me since then that I have no regrets. I do however get envious and sad sometimes when the raw emotion comes out and I just wish I could go to the bathroom with no medical devices. I wish I wasn't like this.

I have had many medical procedures that have taken a toll on me physically since then. Tests and more tests but each one reveals no real hope for help. There is not much the doctors can do besides maintain the condition I am in and try to help me through medication and their best advice when I visit them for my check ups. A day at the doctor entails disappointment almost every time. What I wish to hear from the doctors is that you are well! You are healthy! You don't need any more surgeries or medical equipment to survive! It feels like a death sentence when I do not hear those words.

It takes me quite some time after one of those disappointing doctor's appointments to get a grip, and as so many others will say, put my big girl panties on and deal with it. It is not in the big girl panties that I deal with it, although comically speaking, I wish I could say that it would help! It is in God and in FAITH that my spirit gets ready for the next moment. My hopes seem to be crushed almost daily by the physical injuries my body has sustained from the loss of our son, Matthew. But just as I wrote that last sentence, William, our beautiful gift from God comes in and says, "hey mama," then lays his sweet head on my shoulder and walks right back out of the room. What the devil may try to keep down, God has His special way of bringing back up!

Battle Scars

The "battle scars" all over my body do not symbolize the remnants of a car accident or recreational play, they symbolize the tragic day when I lost my son. Each time I see the scars or the damage from the injury that has come upon me, I remember that day. Not one moment goes by that my body does not feel the pain, the loss of muscle, and the agony of neuropathy. I get so tired of pain and the pretending to the world around me that all is well, physically. I don't want to complain, I don't want pity and I certainly do not wish to hear "poor Lori." So what I have learned to do quite successfully is slap a smile on and be someone who looks so normal on the outside that no one will know the real pain I live with on the inside, physically or emotionally.

It's on my worst of days that I try the hardest to hide the pain. Even to those who love me the most, I hide the hurt from them. Why I do this is actually a very simple answer. I know my loved ones have suffered greatly with the loss of Matthew and they have seen me suffer through so much medically, that I do not want them to see me hurt when they do not have to. If I can control what emotions and pain that I am experiencing when in their presence, I do. I know that if they see me hurting, it will cause them to experience pain. So unless I am in the hospital bed or down where it cannot be camouflaged, I do my very best to remain strong and smile… through it all.

This however, I do not recommend for anyone going through an emotional or painful experience. Those who love you want nothing more than to be there for you. I've learned that. It took me some years and I still try to fake a "yes ma'am, I am fine." But it doesn't fly anymore. It is as if a burden has been lifted where I can admit that I am just having a really bad day. Instead of feeling like I am a burden to those who love me, I must allow them to support me on those bad days. I need that. I've needed that all along, but by thinking I was protecting them from pain, I was actually inflicting more pain upon myself and on them.

My disappointment with life caused me to almost lose myself in grief and anger and pain. It's like I lost myself the day I lost my son. I lost my life as I knew it, I lost my health, I lost my career and my dignity. I was a shell, a very empty broken shell. I didn't know who I was. I remember vividly staring at myself in the mirror not recognizing myself, wondering where did I go? What happened to me? I remember saying over and over, but I just went in to have a baby...

Forgiveness

I was full of anger, guilt and my disappointments had turned into unforgivenenss. Forgiveness is perhaps the hardest lesson to learn when you are in the midst of a tragedy; forgiving a friend, a loved one, but the most challenging of all is forgiving yourself. If you feel like the victim, it is even harder to see why you must forgive. But if there is one thing I've learned as I've walked through these past few years, is forgiveness is a vital part of the healing process. Without forgiveness the heart can not recover and begin to love again. The Bible says we are to love our neighbor as we love ourselves.[21] It is very hard to love if we can't forgive.

Are you in a place where you need to forgive yourself? Do you continually ask yourself if you could have somehow stopped this tragedy? Do you replay the events that led up to the tragedy and try to think of ways you could have saved a life? Do you struggle with guilt thinking there was something you missed that might have prevented those hurtful things from happening? I have struggled with all of the above and I know it is not easy. It is without a doubt a struggle, perhaps the most important battle you will have to face in life. I have come to realize that until I could forgive myself, I

---

[21] See Matthew 19:19

couldn't forgive others. In the Book of Matthew Jesus tells us that if we forgive others our Father will forgive us, but if we do not forgive others, then our Father will not forgive our sins.[22]

Think about this: Is anyone worth keeping you out of heaven? Here's another thought: How much forgiveness do you want and need from God? Jesus said God our Father can only forgive us as much as we forgive others. When we harbor unforgiveness, it allows other stuff to grow in our hearts like anger, bitterness and rage. These all lead to self destruction, self doubt, insecurity and a feeling of unworthiness. Walls are put up and our hearts are hardened, leading us away from love and off of the path that God has chosen for us.

Only when we are in God's will, which means we are doing things God's way, can we have security, peace and fulfillment in our lives. It is only then that we feel worthy to be "God's chosen" and can hold our heads high knowing that our next step is ordered of God and that His goodness and mercy shall follow us all the days of our lives.[23] When we are not aligned with His will, we find ourselves not feeling worthy of God's grace, therefore forgiving ourselves and others seem unattainable and impossible. The devil wants to keep us here because we will eventually self destruct and be of no use to the Kingdom of God if we remain filled with disappointment and unforgiveness.

Chances are, we don't deserve His grace, but God gives it freely! When we are able to accept grace in our lives, and understand that His grace is sufficient, forgiveness has a way of working its way into our hearts. Our hearts will begin to soften as we open our hearts to the goodness of God and we come to realize that if He can forgive us for all we have done, we must be truly loved by Him.

Setting the Captive Free

Forgiveness is the first step to healing. That may sound insignificant to you, but if you take a look at the tragedy that has you in a bind and go all the way to the core of it you will find there is someone or perhaps yourself that you need to forgive. Maybe you will find you have to quit blaming God for what you are experiencing.

---

[22] See Matthew 6:14-15

[23] See Psalm 25

I had to forgive myself for the death of my son. I blamed myself for not knowing he was in danger, not being able to protect him... this led me to believe that I wasn't worth living. Why did I live and he die? I felt unworthy to live, to laugh. I suffered for so long with unforgiveness in my heart. It hurt me more than it hurt anyone else and affected my daily decisions. Proverbs 4:23 says, "Guard your heart above all else, for it determines the course of your life."[24]

When the day came that I was able to forgive myself and others against whom I held unforgiveness, I knew that struggle was over. I read somewhere that when you forgive someone you set a prisoner free. I realized that prisoner was me all along. Unforgiveness will hurt us forever; leading us to disastrous places we don't belong and don't want to be. But forgiveness leads to healing, and healing leads to peace. God wants us to live in peace with others and with ourselves. We are to seek peace with others, with ourselves.

In order to forgive, I had to let go of my pride. I had to humble myself before Jesus and admit my heart was wrong, my intentions were wrong and that I was sorry. I wanted others to hurt because I hurt. I wanted others to understand the pain I suffered everyday, mentally and physically. In reality, after forgiveness made its way into my heart, I knew I didn't want anyone to suffer or hurt. I slowly began to feel compassion coming back and when I saw hurting people I wanted to make it better for them. I was convicted; I repented and was now ready for God to use me to help others on the journey of life and tragedies that come unexpectedly.

The strongest stand I can make on forgiveness is that God forgave you and me for nailing His Son to the cross so that we may have forgiveness for our sins and attain eternal life. Who am I not to forgive someone that has hurt me? Who am I not to forgive myself if Jesus has already paid the price of my sin? God works that way. It may seem like a simple step, but I believe forgiveness is the hardest step we take and often can be the most important on our life journey from tragedy to triumph.

---

[24] NLT

Dealing with the Unexpected

Read this powerful passage from Psalm 25 and make it your prayer as you move forward on your life's journey. Underline the passages that minister to your heart.

UNTO YOU, O Lord, do I bring my life. O my God, I trust, lean on, rely on, and am confident in You. **Let me not be put to shame or [my hope in You] be disappointed;** *let not my enemies triumph over me. Yes, let none who trust and wait hopefully and look for You be put to shame or be disappointed; let them be ashamed who forsake the right or deal treacherously without cause.*

Show me Your ways, O Lord; teach me Your paths. Guide me in Your truth and faithfulness and teach me, for You are the God of my salvation; for You [You only and altogether] do I wait [expectantly] all the day long.

Remember, O Lord, Your tender mercy and loving-kindness; for they have been ever from of old. Remember not the sins (the lapses and frailties) of my youth or my transgressions; according to Your mercy and steadfast love remember me, for Your goodness' sake, O Lord.

Good and upright is the Lord; therefore will He instruct sinners in [His] way. He leads the humble in what is right, and the humble He teaches His way. **All the paths of the Lord are mercy and steadfast love, even truth and faithfulness are they for those who keep His covenant and His testimonies.** *For Your name's sake, O Lord, pardon my iniquity and my guilt, for [they are] great.*

Who is the man who reverently fears and worships the Lord? Him shall He teach in the way that he should choose. **He himself shall dwell at ease, and his offspring shall inherit the land.** *The secret [of the sweet, satisfying companionship] of the Lord have they who fear (revere and worship) Him, and He will show them His* *covenant and reveal to them its [deep, inner] meaning. My eyes are ever toward the Lord, for He will pluck my feet out of the net.*

[Lord] turn to me and be gracious to me, for I am lonely and afflicted. The troubles of my heart are multiplied; bring me out of my distresses. Behold my affliction and my pain and forgive all my sins [of thinking and doing]. Consider my enemies, for they abound; they hate me with cruel hatred. O keep me, Lord, and deliver me; let me not be ashamed or disappointed, for my trust and my refuge are in You. Let integrity and uprightness preserve me, for I wait for and expect You. (AMP)

Chapter Nine

Nathan Lee Weatherly

❦

I will say my biggest source of encouragement has come from Nathan, who was just 5 years old when tragedy stuck our family. He held his baby brother while I was in surgery not understanding the life changing event that he had just witnessed. He has been beside me praying when I am in bed sick since I have come home from the hospital. The days when I had no faith, he would be the light that flickered in the darkness. Even at his young age, God gave him great big faith; a faith that understood that with Christ we can do all things. Perseverance was Nathan's favorite word to say to me. Mama, you just have to persevere! That faith and perseverance has grown and become something we are so proud of.

Just a few weeks ago after a procedure I had that left me in the bed for some time, he crawled in the bed with me. I told him I wanted to talk to him and asked him if I ever disappointed him because I was sick so much. He told me no, not at all and that he understood I had to recover. Then in the same breath he told me rather sternly, "Mama, even on days you don't feel like it, you just got to keep on swinging the bat!" With a smile he hugged me and I knew I had to keep on swinging!

The Compassionate Encourager

Nathan has a heart of compassion for everyone. When he was just 2 years old, he began to notice homeless people on the street. About the age of 3, he prayed for the homeless every night and then we started filling shoeboxes up with food and toiletries for the homeless. We would give them away when we would see one on the corner or under a bridge. On cold, wintery nights Nathan would be so concerned for people who were homeless that he would just pray and pray. I had never seen anything like it; his prayer life at the age of 3 was amazing. He never forgot a need either. We have video of him praying for a sweet teenager from our church that was being tested for cancer. Months after being diagnosed cancer free, he was still praying for her, without our prompting him.

Nathan was named after Nathan the prophet in the Bible, and interestingly enough, in Hebrew Nathan means, "he gave."

When Nathan was in kindergarten, he said he was going to be a preacher and his church was going to be called, The BIG Church. We asked him why BIG? What does that mean? He said it was to be a **Believe In God** Church! At such a young age, he knew that it wasn't religion that mattered; it was his belief and faith in God! He preaches everyday, not on a platform in a church, but at school and at the ball field... not with a sermon, but with a lifestyle. He will take the time to encourage anyone and everyone that needs it.

At his ballgames, my heart smiles when one of his teammates strikes out and as they walk back into the dugout, Nathan is quick to pat them on the shoulder and tell them, "That's okay, you can do it next time; you can do all things through Christ." When he makes a mistake on the field or strikes out and has a hard time shaking it off, I do the encouraging that he does for the other kids. Sometimes I just say, "Moose." He gives me a nod and that is our signal for him to say Philippians 4:13 and get back in the game!

Facets of Life

I am one loud, proud mama that cheers for her Moose! Whether he is in the outfield or behind home plate, he knows where I am because he can hear me screaming for him! He likes to freak his dad out by being a 2 strike hitter! The thought of the 3rd strike pushes him to hit that ball! He is committed to be the best ballplayer and teammate he can be. On the football field, he gets the job done whether on the offensive line or the defensive line! Mama loves to watch him pancake those boys! He also likes to get those sacks as linebacker! Mama likes that too!:)

He is incredibly smart and excels in academics. We are so proud of him for making such good grades and for his many accomplishments in school. He strives to do his best always and is really hard on himself when he doesn't meet "his standard" of excellence.

Katie Warren, his Principal at West Hancock Elementary School says of Nathan, "*I have known Nathan Lee Weatherly for about three years, first as his principal, but more recently as a pastor's wife. He is the epitome of what every parent wants in a son and every teacher wants in a student. It is my pleasure to watch as he grows academically and spiritually. Nathan is a positive child who is blessed with a sharp mind and a delightful personality. He is one of those students that I will never forget. What a joy is it to call Nathan and his family friends. May God bless this wonderful family!*

Nathan looks at all things through eyes of faith. He doesn't see what is there, but rather what is not there. He has what I have heard referred to as "now faith." Hebrews 11:1 says, *"Now faith is being sure of what we hope for and certain of what we do not see."* On my worst of days, he makes me smile; not because of what he does, but because of who he is. Who he is in Christ is by far what we are most proud of. We tell him all of the time that no matter how successful he is academically or on the ball field, what will always remain his best attribute to us and what we are most proud of is his faith in God.

A Little Piece of Heaven

What is incredible for us to see unfolding in front of us is Nathan's ability to talk about heaven and Matthew's death to Will. Will listens intently and is careful to understand the best he can. One day we were at the cemetery and Will wanted to see Matthew in the ground. Nate put his arm around him as he pointed to the sky and said, "Will, heaven is up there, way beyond the clouds and one day we are going, but not today, not until God is ready for us." Will said, "Oh, okay..." and together they walked off to look for lizards! The very next time we visited the cemetery, Will brought his binoculars. Puzzled, but not asking why, I began to do my usual cleaning out there. A few minutes later, I looked up and saw Will standing behind Matthew's monument, sweat running down his forehead as he was holding those little green binoculars to his eyes looking in the sky. I asked him what he was doing. He said "Mom, I am looking for Matthew." Savoring the sweetness of this moment, I searched for the words to say to him, but Nathan didn't waste a second. He jumped in and once again used his big brother status to trump any answer I could have given. What could I do but smile? Sometimes being slow to respond produces the answer that we so desperately need to hear... What a precious memory.

We had no choice in explaining heaven and death to Nathan at a young age... but what I see with Will is that heaven is just part of our every day talk. Our family time always includes Matthew and we often talk about the day we are all going to get to see him again. I love seeing the relationship that the 3 of my boys are building... literally all 3 of them! Will loves Matthew just as he loves Nathan and Nathan loves Will just as much as he loves Matthew. It is beautiful, a little piece of heaven right here for us!

In school just recently, the class had to make hats that would describe who they were. Nathan's hat had a baseball and a football because he loves sports; it has the colors red and blue because they are his favorite colors; it has a light bulb because he said he is smart; and a book because he likes to read; the word History is printed on it because that's favorite subject... but on the top, the very top and standing high above all of the others, there stood a cross. I asked him why the cross was like that. He said "Mama, because Jesus is above everything else I do, always." (Insert a BIG mama grin!)

For the yearbook, Nathan had to write three sentences that describe who he is. The first one said that he played football and baseball. The second one said he liked to ride his four-wheeler, his bike and play with Dixie, our dog in his free time. The last sentence said, I believe I can do all things through Christ who strengthens me. When I told him that was awesome, he said, "Well Mama, don't you think that describes me best?" I told him I couldn't have said it better! That's my boy, that's my Moose! That's what I am most proud of.

February 2, 2011, as I was writing the chapters for this book, I had to take Nathan to the doctor's. He had been suffering with chronic headaches all month so his doctor suggested that we put him on blood pressure medication twice daily and ordered an MRI for him. I had a severe mommy moment and when we got in the car to drive home, I started to cry. Nathan put his arm on my shoulder, looked at me and said, "Mama, don't you worry, I don't like to see you worry. It sounds to me like your fear is clobbering your faith!"

I looked at him and just smiled as a tear fell down my cheek... not because of worry either, but because God has given me such a precious gift of encouragement through my son. This has to do with his own health... he was still encouraging me!

Then he said "Mom, you have to leave the results up to God and know He is taking care of me."

Humbly, I sat there in awe at what had just transpired...I am so thankful for the blessing of the gift Nate has to speak faith into not just his own life, but to everyone around him, especially me! By the way, Nate's MRI was great. Nothing showed, just confirmed his sinus and ears were fine. He has started wearing a night guard to sleep since he has shown evidence of teeth grinding which could be the cause of the migraines. Since he has been wearing it, his headaches have reduced at least 70 percent!

Nathan Lee Weatherly, a gift of life that gives me motivation, determination, encouragement and joy. The gift of faith he has is incredible, but above all else he is unwavering in any situation, expected or unexpected. I asked my friend the other day was it bad for me to say when I grow up I hope I am like my son? I strive to have that kind of faith, the faith of my child.

Thank you sweet Jesus for Nathan and for the blessing that he is to us. Through his words You minister to my heart daily and I know that You have given him a very special gift. May You continue to use him for Your glory and may his faith withstand the storms of life through it all as he grows into the man You are making him to be. We are so grateful for him.

Ronnie on Nathan:

In Luke 18:15-17, people were bringing babies to Jesus to have Him touch them. When the disciples saw this, they rebuked these parents, but Jesus called the children to Him and said, "Let the children come to me, and do not hinder them, for the kingdom of God belongs to such as these. I tell you the truth; anyone who will not receive the kingdom of God like a little child will never enter it."[25] I have heard this verse many times throughout my life and I have always thought I understood its meaning. However, it took Nathan to teach the depth of what Jesus was trying to tell His disciples.

Nathan and I have had a special relationship, especially since July 2, 2005. My love for Nathan didn't change that day but our relationship was impelled to strengthen as our dependence on each other grew. It was four days later before I felt comfortable enough

---

[25] NIV

to leave Lori's side at the hospital. I had spent my nights on the cold floor in the ICU while Nathan was staying with our sisters. When he visited, I could tell the stress was hard on him and that he never wanted to leave Lori or me. On that fourth day, Nathan met me at the hospital and we went out together for dinner and to spend some time together.

It was very surreal that night. I found myself wondering if this was how life may be without my wife. Lori was stable in the hospital but her future was still uncertain. I decided to take Nathan to play miniature golf and ride a few rides at a local amusement park. During those moments Nathan comforted me. His thoughts on Lori were always positive. That evening while dining together, father and son, Nathan had an opportunity to share something with our waitress that gave me insight as to how he was handling all that had transpired in our lives the last four days.

Being friendly, our waitress inquired how we were doing. Nathan had no hesitation in telling her about the circumstances we were in. The waitress was completely caught off guard and began to tear up. Nathan instantly told her it would be okay, "My brother Matthew is now in heaven and my mom, well, she will be home soon because that is how I prayed."

He knew Lori was coming home soon. Why? He told us; because he prayed and believed God would restore our family. It didn't matter what the circumstances were, he simply believed it to be true. Several times during that night I would find myself tearing up, he would grab my hand and tell me it was okay because he had prayed. This didn't reduce the pain. Our family was still broken but it reminded me that we rest our hope in God and in His plans for our life.

Nathan's faith was unshakeable. There were no options of wavering from what he believed. I prayed hard that night that I could also have that childlike faith he possessed. The verse mentioned above seems quite simple. However, if we could only grasp the notion of what Jesus was trying to tell his disciples and tell us as well, the implications are tremendous. The idea of living a life with no fear, no worry, no asking why; instead, this verse implies we can live a life of hope. We must accept His kingdom just as a child accepts a gift, believing in Jesus Christ as our Savior and as our hope; no matter what.

We ended that night at a local souvenir shop. There I allowed Nathan to pick out a few things for his mom. In true Nathan style he bought her a regular sized coffee cup for her and a mini coffee cup for him (in order for them to share their morning coffee together) and a Mardi Gras style necklace, all of which contained logos of Ole Miss. He was so proud to give these things to Lori the next day. Lori still has the gifts from him, but it was the gift Nathan gave me that night in his childlike faith that I will hold forever.

Nathan's thoughts:

Now I enjoy more than ever having my mom at the ball fields with me, because I know it is a miracle for her to be there. I am grateful that she is there and I don't take for granted just having my parents in my life anymore, or my brothers. I realize it is a very, very special thing to have 2 brothers in my life and in my heart and parents that are healthy. Well, my mom isn't so healthy but she is able to be there for me.

We love to play Monopoly together before bed at night. Our prayer time is pretty crazy since Will has been able to pray on his own. He likes to control how we pray and tell us what to pray for. It is good to be able to laugh with a brother by my side at prayer time. He makes me smile even when I have had a bad day.

Today I still love helping homeless people; I don't think I will ever outgrow that. God has given me joy, peace, compassion, and happiness. I try to encourage everyone on the ball field, in school and everywhere else I go. I will always keep the faith and courage that God has given me from the experiences I have had, for they have impacted my faith tremendously. That experience was the most stressful thing I have been through. I was worried that my mom might pass away when she was in the hospital. But I knew to pray.

The feeling of giving to the less fortunate is the greatest feeling I have ever experienced. That feeling is the joy that God has given me. One year for Christmas, my Nana and Pop gave me $45.00 to give to a cause or a less fortunate person. I used the money to buy a homeless family water, dog food for their dog and I gave the rest of the money to them. The homeless man hugged me with tears in his eyes and said "thank you." The joy of God really moved me in that moment. I want to do that all of the time. Even when I am sad I have learned to keep my head up and know that everything will be fine because God is in control. The best thing I could ever give to someone would be the joy of God. The joy of the Lord is my strength.

I try my best to excel in academics and I try to spread the Word of God around school. I know that through my actions, my faith in God will show and it will affect someone tremendously. God has given me the ability to achieve some really cool academic awards and sports awards. I recently placed 3rd in the Academic Competition for Excellence for the Social Studies category. I was so excited! The competition had schools from the Alabama coast and Mississippi coast. I thank Jesus for allowing me to do such an amazing feat. At the Ole Miss Baseball Summer Camp in 2009, I won the Will to Win Award for the 2nd, 3rd and 4th grade division. That was a God moment for me for sure because He gave me strength and encouragement to try my hardest and hustle as the coaches said. I want to be the best I can be and please God with whatever I can do for Him.

God is the most important part of my life. All things are possible with God, and I don't know what I will be doing next year or when I grow up, but I will be doing it with God by my side.

William Gray Weatherly

William Gray, AKA the "Stitch," is a true blessing to all of us! His entry into our hearts started long before he was even born! Will is full of life and laughs! Lots of laughs! He is incredibly gifted in music! He has a stage set up complete with a drum set, 3 amps, 4 guitars (2 electric, 2 acoustic,) and 2 keyboards, a microphone and many other items that make our family room his personal jam session room! He likes rock-n-roll clothes and we cannot rip his jeans up enough for him! He's a mess! He is a bit (a lot) like me in the fashion world and I take credit or blame for that, but he is so stinking cute!

He is taking drum lessons and is really very good! We cannot believe the natural ability God has given to him. We are so proud of him and of the little boy he is. He loves to rock it out any time! It's his passion, music! Just tonight we were singing worship songs as he played his guitar. Ronnie and I looked at each other and in that moment just smiled, sometimes words aren't necessary. God has had a plan for his life since conception... and music is part of that life.

Before Will, we danced... sometimes in the rain, sometimes in the quietness of the night just to be close to each other, but now we dance with a song in our heart and Will's music in our ears. There is no sweeter sound than to hear, "I worship you..." accompanied by our 4-year-old son on his electric guitar. He is unique and one of a kind! He has an eye for detail and doesn't miss a thing... not a thing! He is a character that we love to watch, but most importantly he is our gift from God and we are so grateful for his song!

We look forward to what is to come and for the journey that he is taking us on. His curiosity of heaven keeps us on our toes, his love for his brother Matthew keeps us on our knees. He ponders every word spoken about Matthew and is quick to dig for more details. He wants to go to heaven all the time. Mercy, there is no definition of love that would be adequate to describe how much we love him. He is certainly a very special little boy that God has used to give us back the song and the music that we longed for. He is not just one handful... but 2 handfuls... Thank God we have a village, because it takes one to help raise him! ☺

Special Note on My Boys:

The sweetest moments of pregnancy with both of my boys would later teach me a valuable lesson within. Every day I would place my hands upon my belly and sing that sweet little children's song, "He's still working on me, to make me what I ought to be. It took him just a week to make the moon and the stars, the sun and the earth and Jupiter and Mars. How loving and patient He must be... He's still working on me."

All the while, He was working on me too... and to this very day, He still is. I will always be a work in progress, a work that was started in my mother's womb, just as He did with Nathan, Matthew and Will. Jeremiah 1:5 says, "Before I formed you in the womb, I knew you, before you were born, I set you apart."

Thank you, Lord for still working on me... to make me what I ought to be, for setting me apart...

Being confident of this, that He who began a good work in you, will carry it on to completion. (Philippians 1:6)

Dealing with the Unexpected

Nathan, Matthew and Will have taught us innumerable lessons on faith, hope and love especially when we are faced with the unexpected circumstances of life. In Luke 18:15-17, Jesus taught the principle of child-like faith. He was also instructing us as parents how to encourage this faith. Read this passage and then record what you have learned.

Now they were also bringing [even] babies to Him that He might touch them, and when the disciples noticed it, they reproved them. But Jesus called them [the parents] to Him, saying, Allow the little children to come to Me, and do not hinder them, for to such [as these] belongs the kingdom of God. Truly I say to you, whoever does not accept and receive and welcome the kingdom of God like a little child [does] shall not in any way enter it [at all]. (AMP)

Jesus talks about another area our children often excel over us in Matthew 21:16. Read this passage and allow true praise for your Heavenly Father to rise up in you. Give your heart over to the song of joy He has placed within you.

And Jesus replied to them, Yes; have you never read, Out of the mouths of babes and unweaned infants You have made (provided) perfect praise? (AMP)

Chapter Ten

Happiness is Circumstantial, Joy is God-Given

※

There are many life lessons I have learned over the past five years. If anyone asked me (and they have) would I do it all over again knowing the outcome of what has happened, my answer with no hesitation, is YES! Yes, I would. I love what Matthew has taught me without ever speaking a word to me. I don't like the circumstances. I don't like the physical pain and emotional pain, but I love knowing that I am Matthew's mama!

I appreciate all of the things that I once took for granted. I see things maybe some others do not see in the most unusual of places, like wildflowers. Have you ever thought about where and how wildflowers grow? I began to notice these beautiful flowers on days when I was at my lowest. I would see that on the ugliest of roads, in the dirtiest of places, in the most unlikely bends of a broken road, God will place a beautiful wildflower. To me, that signifies hope. He is there. He can make something beautiful out of anything, anywhere. He can bring His magnificent splendor and make it grow in the middle of trash. We can pick it and walk away. Or we can admire it from afar and say thank you God for such beauty in the midst of the ashes and allow it to be a building block of faith in our life. By leaving the wildflower there, someone else can come along and experience the beauty in that moment of their lives when they just may need it the most. We all need wildflowers.

Don't Let Anyone Steal Your Joy

I have learned that even on my saddest of days when I can't seem to find any happiness in anything around me, I can still have joy. **Happiness is circumstantial, yet joy is God-given**. Happiness is based on what is going on around me. A rainy day can make me feel sad while a bright sunny day makes me feel happy. Seeing what I can't do, can bring in waves of sadness while wiggling my big toe can produce a wave of strong hope. A discouraging doctor's report used to ruin my day but I have realized God can give me joy no matter what the weather is like or the doctor's tell me is impossible to fix.

My husband has shown me the secret to true joy and what unconditional love is as I have never known it before. He has stood beside me, lay beside me, cried with me, and let me scream at him in utter frustration. He has held me through every circumstance we have gone through all the while telling me, we can do this together moment by moment with God. He has taught me a great lesson in handling the unexpected circumstances we have had to face in life. It is so easy for me to become overwhelmed, but Ronnie has broken it down to manageable moments. He knows that to get me through this moment, I cannot think about the next.

His support has been incredible and God has blessed me by giving me such a gift of a husband who truly exhibits God's unconditional love. Ronnie tells me all of the time, **"Don't let anyone steal your joy."** Ironically just last week, we were at the pain management doctor and he pointed to a sign that said, "Don't let anyone steal your joy." He reminds me that I always have a choice as to how much I will allow the unexpected events of life to affect my joy. I have come to realize the amazing truth of Nehemiah 8:10 which says, "Do not grieve, for the joy of the Lord is your strength."[26]

Clinging to Ashes

Clinging to the ashes of what once was or what could have been only causes smut to reside all over you. Trying to remove the residue left on your skin from the ashes seems like an endless endeavor. No matter how much physical strength or mental determination we have, we cannot remove the stains left on our skin. But when we grab a bottle of cleanser and begin to scrub our hands, we begin to see the surface of the skin that once was free of ashes. We may even experience some discomfort as the cleanser works on our skin to remove the deeply embedded stains.

Isaiah 61:3 speaks of what God sent Jesus to the earth to accomplish in His people, "To grant [consolation and joy] to those who mourn in Zion—to give them an ornament (a garland or diadem) of **beauty instead of ashes**, the oil of **joy instead of mourning**, the garment [expressive] of praise instead of a heavy, burdened, and failing spirit—that they may be called oaks of righteousness [lofty, strong, and magnificent, distinguished for uprightness, justice, and right standing with God], the planting of the Lord, that He may be glorified."[27]

In that same manner, God will take the ashes and the residue left in our hearts that is caused by pain and hurt and cleanse, renew and turn our grieving into joy if we allow Him to do so. Easier said than done; experience has taught me that. I believe that when I have held onto ashes, it is because I feel like they are valuable and if I let them

---

[26] NIV

[27] AMP

go then I no longer possess what treasure I held even though it has turned into ruins. Truth is, God wanted to take those ruins and give me beauty and joy. The next verse in Isaiah actually says that God will help us "rebuild the ancient ruins and renew the ruined cities."[28] It can only be accomplished with God's help, though.

Where Your Treasure Is...

Jesus told His disciples in Matthew 6:21, "Where your treasure is, there your heart will be also."[29] I was treasuring what *used to be*; my health, our son, our expectations of what life was supposed to be. Trying to hold on to what used to be was destructive. It kept me from moving forward into my destiny. It stood in the way of living in the joy of the Lord. It is a terrible thing to hold on to. Jesus said He came to preach the good news, heal the broken-hearted and set the captives free.[30] God's heart is to take those ruins and not only restore but rebuild; maybe not in the way we think we want, though. They may never be the same but they will be done in the way that is according to His word, His plan and His timing.

I have to be honest with you though, I spent many days in my home alone sobbing brokenhearted and crying out to God. I read Isaiah 63:9 which says, "In all their distress, he too was distressed and the angel of his presence saved them. In his love and mercy he redeemed them; he lifted them up and carried them all the days of old."[31] I wanted to be saved, redeemed, lifted up and carried... and when I was ready to allow it, God did just that!

My heart's cry was to remember the time when I left the world, flat lining on the operating table. I longed to know if I had time with Matthew, how long was I in heaven? What did I experience? On one of my most heart wrenching nights, the following words came to me. As I wrote them, my body grew weak and tears flowed from my

---

[28] See Isaiah 61:4
[29] NIV
[30] See Luke 4:18-19 and Isaiah 61:1-4
[31] NIV

body. I knew this was God's way of answering that prayer, through words, as He so often did.

Breath Of Life

Breath of life leaving your body, blood escaping every vein
Leaving you lifeless, lying in pain.
I was screaming at all, why isn't he crying
No one would answer, no one replying.
Instead I hear moans in the room with me,
As life surely came, with death you would leave.
Inside I was screaming, wouldn't you hear?
Was I really dying, were these my last tears?
The tears turned to blood, I was dripping wet.
I was going far away, but I will never forget.
Forget the last moment before I went,
The moment you came, the moment you left.
In my mind I see you gasping for breath,
And I am trying to help you but you enter your death.
I cannot reach you, I am trying so much
You needed me, you needed my touch.
I am close behind you as I too am in pain
For you leaving me it took my breath away.
I quit breathing and gave up on living,
As my body was weak and the blood it was leaving.
The blood it covered me, running out of every pore,
Leaving my body dead at the core.
No one would hear me, I couldn't speak
But I was screaming inside as those around did weep.
Why can't you hear me, what happened to me?
Why did my baby die? I no longer see.
What happened now, where did you all go?
Why can't I feel you, are you letting me go?
Don't go...don't go... stay with me please
I am scared and afraid, where are they taking me?
The blood is flowing all over the place,
Like sweat on my brow, it drenches my face.

God can you hear me? No one else can.
Do you have my baby? Are you holding my hand?
Please give him back for me to keep
Please dear God, take this cup from me.
I don't want to leave You or him right away
Please let me rest and let me stay.
My breath is gone, also my blood
My lifeline has stopped, has Thy will been done?
You are sending me back but I don't want to go
Please Jesus, Please Jesus… okay I will go.
My work is not yet through on the earth I see
And restoration I know You have promised to me.
I will go and do Your work as YOU will
For I know You are in heaven, holding me still.
Holding my son, waiting on me
Until I am called home for eternity…

Just reading those words again, I get emotional but they helped me begin to understand why God allows His people to suffer. I finally quit asking myself why me and started asking why not me? Why not me to be able to touch the heart of another grieving mother? Why not me to be able to understand the needs of so many disabled people? Why not me to be able to relate to someone who is struggling with depression? Why not???

Pain Is…

Pain is what brought me to this place in my life, this journey of heartache and tragedy, the experience of having to let go while desperately trying to hold on. Pain caused a constant struggle for peace and joy leaving me confusion and sorrow. Pain is hard. Pain is constant. Pain is overwhelming both physically and emotionally. Pain is deep; I tried to bury it far away, yet it surfaced again and again as anger, unforgiveness, resentment or the worst of all, rebellion against God. Pain drove me to places I never wanted to go.

When you are in pain, what you are in search of is something to take the pain away, something that will make you forget, or keep you isolated from feeling the intense pain, even if just for a while. But if not dealt with properly, it always returns. Taking care of the inside is far more important then tending to the outside. What you may care about is the outside and masking from the world the pain you feel while your heart is full of pain and suffering. I have done that for years. It's not worth it!

Pain put me in the corner for a very long time, afraid to let others see who I had become. But I know that by sharing my most personal thoughts about my family, my health and the tragedy in our lives, that I could also share with you my testimony. God brings us through tragedy so that we may help others by sharing how we have overcome our trials and tribulations. You may have seen me walking… but did you know there is a miracle behind that? Now you do, and as scared as I was to be vulnerable, I knew that on my journey this was a step of faith I had to take even though I am still enduring pain.

In choosing to share my story with each of you, my prayer would be that you will not focus on the pain that is currently in your life, but that you will see that the benefits of accepting the restoration offered by God, our Heavenly Father, who loves, heals, forgives, protects, and gives grace and mercy to us even when we don't think we are worthy of Him.

Thank you, Jesus for the pain, the longsuffering that is producing in me daily the person that You want me to be. Thank You for the pain that has driven me to the answer, the cross. The cross that You died on for me and for all of us to take our pain, our sins, our transgressions. Thank You for Your unfailing love and Your amazing grace. May You bless the heart of each person reading this and may they know that pain is not the end, but can be beginning of their search for You.

Dealing with the Unexpected

Read this powerful passage from Isaiah 61:1-7 that so ministered to me during my times of deep sadness and overwhelming grief. I pray it ministers to your heart as it did to mine! Underline those portions that are written just for you.

THE SPIRIT of the Lord God is upon me, because the Lord has anointed and qualified me to preach the Gospel of good tidings to the meek, the poor, and afflicted; He has sent me to bind up and heal the brokenhearted, to proclaim liberty to the [physical and spiritual] captives and the opening of the prison and of the eyes to those who are bound, to proclaim the acceptable year of the Lord [the year of His favor] and the day of vengeance of our God, to comfort all who mourn, to grant [consolation and joy] to those who mourn in Zion—to give them an ornament (a garland or diadem) of beauty instead of ashes, the oil of joy instead of mourning, the garment [expressive] of praise instead of a heavy, burdened, and failing spirit—that they may be called oaks of righteousness [lofty, strong, and magnificent, distinguished for uprightness, justice, and right standing with God], the planting of the Lord, that He may be glorified.

And they shall rebuild the ancient ruins; they shall raise up the former desolations and renew the ruined cities, the devastations of many generations. Aliens shall stand [ready] and feed your flocks, and foreigners shall be your plowmen and your vinedressers. But you shall be called the priests of the Lord; people will speak of you as the ministers of our God. You shall eat the wealth of the nations, and the glory [once that of your captors] shall be yours. Instead of your [former] shame you shall have a twofold recompense;

instead of dishonor and reproach [your people] shall rejoice in their portion. Therefore in their land they shall possess double [what they had forfeited]; everlasting joy shall be theirs.

Write your own *thank you prayer* to God for the healing and restoration He is doing in your heart. Thank Him for taking the ashes and replacing them with life. Thank Him for filling your heart with joy, His joy and for the strength His joy gives you to move forward fulfilling your destiny in Him.

Conclusion

One Day At A Time

I am learning to live with chronic pain and continue to see my doctors regularly. I struggle with strength in my left leg due to the muscle degeneration and atrophy that the nerve damage has caused. The back pain I have is unbearable on most days, but I am learning to grin and bear it... okay, so maybe not always grinning while bearing it. Medications are used to help with the neuropathy and the pain. It's not easy. Each day presents new challenges. I am reminded of the Israelites when they were in the desert and God would provide them just enough manna for the day. God wanted them to depend upon HIM daily to meet their needs. At the end of every day I realize God has always met my need, calmed my fear, and carried me through to the next.

I often think of my future five years from now. Will I be walking? Will I be running? No one knows, but Jesus. He is the author of all life and I am so thankful that He allowed me to live, to be a mom, a wife, a daughter, a sister and a friend.

Although I am physically handicapped, and the stamina in my legs is not what it used to be, I do all that I can to enjoy life together with my family. Don't think for a second a few weeks ago when my boys wanted to go ice skating that I didn't try... Not only did I try, I skated as if I could feel both of my legs and feet! As Ronnie and I locked eyes upon each other, I squeezed his hand, he returned the squeeze and we both knew it was a miracle; another notch in my mommy belt of not missing something that my boys wanted to do.

What would seem impossible for someone like me to do, I did! I don't want to sit on the sidelines of life; I want to strap my skates on and get out there and play! Play with my boys and make memories! Of course, I paid for it for 2 days after laying in the bed on the heating pad... but worth it, yes, oh so worth it! I know my limits; I know what will keep me in bed for a couple of days until I can bounce back, and I am very aware the importance of making those decisions. Spending a few hours at the ball field is a risk every time I go, but I am not about to miss it. Pain for me in the moment or tomorrow is well worth my boys' smile today.

Next on my 'bucket list...' snow skiing! Yes indeed! At least once! I may have to end the vacation on a tube sliding down the hill, but I will ski! I have already perfected the art of lying in the sun and on the pool raft... My boys think I am the best at that!

Truth is, doctors do not expect me to get any better... they are just expecting to help me cope with life and help me to be as comfortable as I can and to maintain quality of life as long as I can. The nerve damage that I have is so extensive and as the aging process is inevitable, so are the degeneration of muscles and bones. There are always talks of surgeries, medications, shots and more... very sobering talks that overwhelm me easily.

A talk that is fresh on my mind since we just had one like that this morning with the doctor. Following the doctor visit, we went to eat lunch to celebrate Valentine's Day. Knowing I was a bit on edge and very close to tears, Ronnie took my hand, looked at me as he gently reminded me, "one moment at a time..." (sigh) and then he ordered me a BIG dessert!

With each day comes uncertainty, but it comes with the promise of the One who holds it! We do not know what the future will bring, but we do know what the past has taught us. We know how to hold on to faith when we have nothing else to hold on to. We know how to embrace the moment and live as best we can whatever the circumstance. We know how to dance in the rain, while we wait for the rainbow. We know that God is in control and He has never left us nor forsaken us and He never will.

Without a miracle of complete healing, there will be more surgeries, tests and procedures for me. There will be obstacles and challenges of growing older with the injuries that I have. But along with that there will be more faith and hope, more love and compassion, more strength and weakness, more testimonies and outreach. There will be more of God than there ever will be of me or my circumstances. Greater is He that is in me, than he that is in the world![32]

Psalm 62:5 says, "My soul, wait only upon God and silently submit to Him; for my hope and expectation are from Him" (AMP)

Webster's Dictionary defines **expectation** as the act or state of expecting or looking forward to an event as about to happen. With great expectation we awaited the joy our baby boy would bring. I expected to be overjoyed to become a mommy again. I expected flowers, but not flowers with baby angels attached to them and a black wreath that would hang upon our business door to let all know that the arrival of our second son turned into something we didn't expect, his death. We went from baby blue to black. From sunshine and daisies to mud puddles and gray skies.

---

[32] See 1John 4:4

Today, almost 6 years later, I am careful to know that with expectations, a risk is always there that could lead to disappointment at any given moment. I have had many lessons on that one. But that cannot keep me from expecting good things! God is a giver of good things! Without expectations, what do we have to hope for?

In looking over the tragedy and triumph in our lives since that fateful day on July 2, 2005, I can say that without God we never would have made it! Without faith, we would have never wanted to make it! God has taken this misplaced mother and wife and given me new breath, breath of survival. I stand firm in all that I believe in. I like who I am, and love my Creator for making me into a woman after God's heart. God has taken and refined my mess, refined my heartache, refined my soul and my imperfections. In my weakness, He has made me strong.

When I look into the mirror today, I am proud of the woman I see. I see a woman who has surrendered all to God and can rest knowing that He is in control of my life and has ordained my steps. My steps may be painful, emotionally and physically, but I am walking in faith. I recognize that I am a new creation in Christ and I know that who I am today is the woman that He has been working on since I was formed in my mother's womb. From the first steps I took as a little girl, my parents showed me the way to the cross... and although I have gotten off of the path along the way, God has brought me home, to stay. Through my journey, I know that the tender moments I have had with my family and with God have steadied my course and rooted me deeper in my walk of faith.

I don't see the old me, <u>sometimes I miss what she could do</u>... but I no longer miss who she was! I am in Christ, ALL that HE wants me to be. It has taken me these past 6 years to see and understand that. I am not in the corner anymore, I am in a book! It is a book of messes and miracles, a book of life and love, a book of survival and surrender!

Someone asked me the other day what I would like people to remember of me. Of course, my first response was I *know* I will be remembered as a crazy Kodak Mama! (I always have my camera ready to capture a moment, for I know how precious they are.) But after pondering for some time, I said I would *like* for people to remember me as a gracious person, one who not just accepts grace from the Heavenly Father, but one who gives grace to others. A person who has learned to be authentic; real and genuine, flaws and all, and with no doubt a gal with some really fabulous shoes!

If you see God's grace and that I am real, then you have to believe that God is working on me and in me, and perhaps you will be able to accept that grace in your life today. Without God's grace, I would not have been able to write this book. I would be fake smiling, adding an extra coat of lip-gloss and mascara and telling everyone I am fine. Don't let me mislead you... I love lip-gloss and mascara and I think every girl has to have it; I just don't need it to cover up for me anymore! I can smile when I look in the mirror at who I am today.

Philippians 3:12-14 describes me today, "Not that I have already obtained all of this, or have already been made perfect, but I press on to take hold of that for which Christ Jesus took hold of me. Brothers, I do not consider myself yet to have taken hold of it. But one thing I do: forgetting what is behind and straining toward what is ahead. I press on toward the goal to win the prize for which God has called me heavenward in Christ Jesus."[33]

I look forward to the days ahead, because God has them in the palm of His hand. Sure I am afraid when I look with my human eyes at my feet that are so fragile and my legs that are weak. But when I take my eyes off of what I see and the pain I feel and focus on Jesus and the promise He has given to me, fear has no room in my heart. God has not given us a spirit of fear, not yesterday, not today and certainly not tomorrow! I don't expect the sun to shine on a rainy day, but I do expect a rainbow!

This book would not be complete without sharing with you the most famous saying in our home..."We do not remember the days, we remember the moments!" We didn't have days with Matthew, but those moments, we will never forget.

---

[33] NIV

One moment can change your life, forever, as our story tells you. One moment can leave you breathless; it is that moment when you know it has happened... a change. A change that can interpret how your story will be written out... but always remember the author is Our Heavenly Father. How do you want your story to end? Do you want eternal life, peace and joy? Do you want peace in a chaotic world? Although God is the author of all life, He has given you the pen. What will your story say? How will it end?

Then maidens will dance and be glad, young men and old as well. I will turn their mourning into gladness; I will give them comfort and joy instead of sorrow. I will satisfy the priests with abundance, and my people will be filled with my bounty," declares the LORD. This is what the LORD says: "A voice is heard in Ramah, mourning and great weeping, Rachel weeping for her children and refusing to be comforted, because her children are no more." This is what the LORD says: "Restrain your voice from weeping and your eyes from tears, for your work will be rewarded," declares the LORD.

"They will return from the land of the enemy. So there is hope for your future," declares the LORD. *"Your children will return to their own land. I have surely heard Ephraim's moaning: You disciplined me like an unruly calf, and I have been disciplined. Restore me, and I will return, because you are the LORD my God."* (Jeremiah 31:13-18 NIV)

About the Author

Lori Clark Weatherly is a full time stay at home mother where she and her husband Ronnie, of 12 years, currently live in Kiln, Mississippi, with their two boys, 10 year old Nathan and 4 year old William. Lori is active in her children's lives and takes great delight in experiencing the joy they bring to her and her family. Cheering Nathan on at the baseball field or football field and taking Will to drum lessons are indeed her favorite things to do. Although on the outside Lori may appear to be a picture of health, she has many medical problems and maintains her medical care at Ochsner in New Orleans, Louisiana, on a regular basis, where she has a wonderful team of doctors there that are always looking for new ways to help her on her physical journey.

Lori is very driven and passionate when it comes to helping women and those families that are in pain, especially those who have experienced the loss of a child. Lori has served on Women's ministry teams at church and post-injury started a Bible Study within her home that met monthly and shared daily devotionals with ladies across the country, as well as prayer requests, and serving those that were in need for about 2 years. She took some time off to recover from a series of surgeries and then a year ago started hosting a Bible Study in her home again on a monthly basis.

Lori has been through much devastation which includes her son passing away the day before her 31st birthday as well as insurmountable physical trauma and injuries. She has experienced loss of much in her life barely having the stamina to stand at times. It was then she has learned to crawl right back to the feet of Jesus. She has certainly learned many life lessons and is looking forward to ministering to others who need to see firsthand how God's grace and mercy have become not just an essential to her and her family, but a necessity.

Learning to love again, live again and find a new normal would prove to be an obstacle that with God's help she and her family are able to overcome on a daily basis. Still today she requires God's help and grace to get her through much of life and depends upon the promise that God has given her of the hope that lies within her heart. God has been so gracious to her, He is the author of all life, and she is grateful He is still working on her story.

Lori Clark Weatherly
FacetsofLife@yahoo.com

Random Acts of Kindness in Memory of Matthew Clark Weatherly

In honor of Matthew's 5th birthday, my dear friend Donna Lively called and told me she heard about an act of kindness card in memory of a loved one. She explained it to me in case I was interested in doing something like this for Matthew. Of course, I was overjoyed at her thoughtfulness and very excited to do such a wonderful thing that would encourage others to be kind to others, when it wasn't expected! A random act of kindness!

We printed 500 cards, and within just a couple of weeks, they were all gone! So many people wanted cards; they literally went all over the U.S. I have heard many wonderful stories of how they have blessed others by doing acts of kindness! And then learning how they have been blessed by doing so. It has been awesome to do and incredible to know that kind acts are being done showing God's love in honor of Matthew.

People love to give and to bless others, and with this motivation it is an awesome reminder to do just that. I love the legacy that these cards are leaving state by state... someone is being blessed and that makes my heart happy.

But you don't need a card to do something for someone! Honor God by giving your time, your care and your love to someone in need, or pay for their meal when they are behind you in the drive thru line; that is always unexpected! I promise you will be blessed!

We gave out the cards and just asked that the cardholder do an act of kindness, and give that person the card, then that person is asked to pay it forward. (see what is printed on the cards below). If you would like some cards, you can email us at the address below! This is an awesome way to show God's love without saying a word.

Random Acts of Kindness in Honor of Matthew Clark Weatherly

Jesus said, "I tell you the truth, anything you did for the least of my people here, you did it for me." Matthew 25:40

In honor of our precious son, we hope to touch your heart with this simple act of kindness. If you have received this card, please keep it going by paying it forward to someone else. If this card has reached you, please email us at: InMemoryofMatthewClarkWeatherly@yahoo.com

CPSIA information can be obtained at www.ICGtesting.com
Printed in the USA
BVOW08s1517290813

329872BV00004B/51/P